The Celtic Wheel of Life

A Path to Health, Happiness and Fulfilment

Andy Baggott

Gateway

Gateway
an imprint of
Gill & Macmillan Ltd
Hume Avenue
Park West
Dublin 12

with associated companies throughout the world
www.gillmacmillan.ie

© 2000 Andy Baggott
0 7171 2957 8
Print origination by Carole Lynch
Printed by ColourBooks Ltd, Dublin

A catalogue record is available for this book
from the British Library.

3 5 4

This book is dedicated to my partner, Debbie,
who has continually challenged me over the past ten years
to find the wisdom within myself. I thank her for her
patient support, gentle teaching and beauty.

CONTENTS

Acknowledgements   vi

Introduction   vii

Chapter One   The Spiral of Life   1

Chapter Two   The Four Elements   17

Chapter Three   The Wheel of the Year   41

Chapter Four   Finding True Balance   70

Chapter Five   Celtic Tree Medicine   93

Chapter Six   Celtic Animal Medicine   124

Chapter Seven   The Power of the Land   150

Chapter Eight   Respect and the Power of Ceremony   170

Chapter Nine   The Celtic Sweatlodge   191

Bibliography and further reading   209

ACKNOWLEDGEMENTS

I would like to thank all the friends I have made along the path, especially those who have shared ceremony with me. Especial thanks go to Debbie for proof-reading and inspiration, Eli for his friendship, my parents Jean and Michael Baggott for their unfailing support and Debbie's parents Jean and John Blackaby for their continual encouragement. Thanks also go to Laura, Freyja, Sue, Jen, Ernesto Alvarado, Eliana Harvey, Dennis Renault, Chris, Jim and Siobhan and appreciation to David Madden for sharing his tale of St. Feichin. I would also like to acknowledge the support of my agent, Susan Mears and Michael Alcock at Gill & Macmillan for commissioning this project.

INTRODUCTION

I write this introduction having just finished writing the final chapter of this book. I chose to leave the writing of this until the end because it marks the end of a process for me and the beginning of a new one for you, the reader. This ideally demonstrates the underlying theme that runs throughout this work — that death is life and life is death. Having written this book, I now need to let it go, to die to it so that my words can be reborn in your mind. As you learn about the Celtic Wheel of Life you will learn the nature of the universe and the power and teachings of both life and death. You will learn not to judge but to accept everything with pleasure so that challenging cycles of learning can unfold naturally without causing you distress. This is a book about happiness, health and fulfilment in every aspect of life *and* death.

So much has been written about the Celts and Celtic shamanism — so what makes this book different? Well, I study the Celtic spiritual path but I also walk it every day of my life. I have, for the past ten years, made it my journey to discover the real power and magic of the Celts. As a child, I was always enthralled by Celtic myth and legend and spent a great deal of time dreaming of magicians and heroes. More than anything else in the world I wanted to believe in magic. As I grew older, my belief in magic slowly waned as the trials and tribulations of young adulthood came upon me. Then, in my mid-twenties I began to search once more for the magic that I sensed existed somewhere in the world. I began to reread books that I had not looked at since I was at school. Books on extra-sensory perception, Celtic myth and legend, Stonehenge and Chinese medicine and philosophy.

I don't remember exactly how or when, but at some stage I understood that I was never going to find what I was searching for in the world around me. It was then that I started to look within myself and tried to understand my place in this wonderful universe. I suddenly realised that all my reading about magic would serve me no purpose. I wanted to experience the magic for myself and to do that I had to start trying to create it myself. It was then that I began to work with ceremony. I found it fascinating yet at the same time a little scary. My Christian upbringing had left me with a great fear of black magic and Satan — I nearly abandoned my path on more than one occasion through fear of Beelzebub and all his hordes coming to take me off to hell. But something inside me made me want to search all the more. Surely a life full of fear and frustration was not the ultimate lot of a human being?

The more I searched within myself, the more answers I attracted into my life. I began to understand that I did not need to go out and search for answers because, if I looked for them within myself, I discovered that I would attract into my life someone or something that would reveal the answer to me. I studied Chinese medicine, traditional herbalism, the four elements, Tai Chi, Taoism, Buddhism and Native American spirituality, always relating what I learnt to myself, trying to integrate their truths into my life. I realised that all the paths contained truths and that it was part of my destiny to bring these truths into my life as a Celt. To understand the Celtic path I have had to study many other paths and, in doing so, I have uncovered many insights and understandings. My two greatest sources of insight came from Chinese and Native American spiritual practices. I learnt a new understanding of energy and the laws of the universe from Chinese martial arts and macrobiotics and from Native American medicine men I learnt about the power of ceremony and the meaning of honour and respect.

I now live and work as a Celtic medicine man treating patients from all over the world with such varied problems as cancer, irritable bowel syndrome, ME, arthritis, rheumatism, eczema, asthma and just about every other common disease. My approach is to teach people how to respect and honour themselves and the land they live upon. I have treated Christians, Buddhists, Pagans,

Jehovah's Witnesses, Jews and Sikhs. I have treated housewives, executives, actors, musicians, travellers, medical professionals, headteachers and many children. I have done no more than share my truth with all of them. This is the wonderful thing about the Celtic path; it is a path of truths. Truth is not dependent upon belief or status, age or origin; it just is. As I have shared these truths I have discovered, and continue to discover, many more. For me, the future is unwritten. I spend no time worrying or thinking about it because I understand that my perspective on the world will continue to change day by day as I learn more about myself and the world around me.

I have found a meaning within the Celtic spiritual path that allows me to walk in this modern world in peace and harmony. I use the knowledge I have accumulated in a very practical and down-to-earth way. I am neither a mystic nor a magician but I now know that mystery, mysticism and magic are within each and every one of us. I am not unusual, nor is my life, but the way I have chosen to perceive this world often makes people think that I might be. What I have in my life, though, this magic and wonderful connection I share with creation, can be yours too if you learn to look within yourself.

One of the things that has always attracted me about the Celtic path is the sense that it is all-embracing. The Celts were nomadic tribesmen who lived off the land. They learnt to utilise all that was available and this included spiritual knowledge. The Celts had no canon of scripture to become indoctrinated to, they lived and learnt through creation around them, embracing everything with pleasure and seeking to learn from every experience. They held on to nothing and rejected nothing realising that there is a middle road of harmony that we can all tread if we so desire.

This book is a collection of some of the things I have learnt from following a Celtic path. It includes a basic model of the universe in terms of the four elements into which anything can be fitted. I make no apology for the fact that I have 'Celticised' some aspects of Chinese medicine and included them in this volume because I am sure that my Celtic ancestors would have done the same. No one tradition has a monopoly on truth and if I find truths in other traditions I add them to my spiritual model. My model happens to be Celtic but it could just as easily have been Native American, Chinese or Buddhist because ultimately there is no Celtic Way, no Native American Way and no Buddhist Way, there is just The Way.

We are all seeking the same truths and this book is my understanding of the truths I have encountered so far on my path through life. There is such depth and diversity within the Celtic world that it would be impossible for me to include every aspect of Celtic spirituality. Instead, I have sought to write a series of studies on the major aspects of the Celtic tradition that have most influenced me. It is a study in connections because the great strength of the Celts was understanding connections. We are all individuals but the spark of creation links us with every atom of the universe and the Celts understood how to harness this power for the benefit of all.

The opening chapter discusses the significance to the Celts of circles and spirals and shows how their understanding of the universe allowed them to interact with creation in a manner that has long been forgotten by most westerners. This leads into a study of the four elements and how they relate to modern living as a model of balance and harmony. This second chapter contains the model I use in my treatment of all modern diseases and shows how our lack of balance physically, emotionally and spiritually is the real cause of illness. This is followed by a series of chapters about how to find balance and harmony again through forming a connection with creation around you. The third chapter is devoted to the cycle of the seasons, the fourth to eating in harmony with the land, the fifth to the energy and teaching of trees and the sixth to animals as guides and teachers on the spiritual path. The seventh chapter looks at the sacred landscape and its meaning both to the Celts and to modern man and this is followed by a chapter of practical teachings on the use of ceremony and ritual for personal empowerment and development. The final chapter focuses on the Celtic sweatlodge and draws upon my personal experience as a shaman leading ceremony and interacting with the energies of the land I live on. This is designed not only to provide an overview of the Celtic tradition, but to show how it is relevant to modern people living in a modern world. Throughout this work I draw on a combination of my personal experience, insights and understandings interwoven with Celtic mythology and spirituality.

What does it mean to follow a Celtic path?

I am sure every follower of the path has their own set of ideas but all the ideas have the same foundation in truth and respect. I have followed a Celtic path for many years now and, the longer I do, the clearer my understanding of my purpose and destiny becomes. I believe it is the destiny of everyone to be happy, healthy and fulfilled, if they choose to seek it. If you are following your soul purpose, you will naturally be happy, healthy and fulfilled. If you seek your own happiness, health and fulfilment, you will naturally be seeking your destiny. I believe that the answers to all questions and the cures to all illnesses lie within the mind of each individual. You have the power within you to find the answers you seek and, with all the help and guidance that creation can offer, there is no limit to what you can achieve. If you can imagine something, you can make it a reality.

In this book I have sought to show you the path I have taken, to share with you the stories that have inspired me and to explain how they relate to me in my everyday life. The Celtic world is a rich landscape of limitless possibilities where you can learn from everything, be it human, animal, plant or stone. If you close your mind to the possibility of other realms of existence, then you deny yourself the wisdom and understanding that can show you how to find happiness, health and fulfilment. However, if you approach this book with an open mind, you will see the world as I see it, a multi-dimensional adventure playground full of fun and profound learning. This does not mean my life is easy — on the contrary, I would say that my life is more challenging now than it has ever been. What the Celtic path has taught me is to embrace everything with pleasure. Even when you are at your weakest and most disempowered, you can still relish the experience safe in the knowledge that you will emerge stronger and wiser because of it. To understand strength, you must first experience weakness. To understand joy, you must first experience pain. Neither is good or bad until you choose how you interact with it. The Celtic path provides an understanding of how processes of learning unfold, allowing one to embrace change rather than fight it.

What does one need to follow a Celtic path?

Firstly, you need a deep-rooted faith — a belief that you are on this planet to learn and grow as spiritual beings and that you are responsible for everything that manifests into your life.

Secondly, you need doubt! How can you have faith and doubt? The doubt I am talking about is a sense of being ever-questioning: why is there so much suffering in the world? what can I do to change that? what are the lessons I need to understand? Without doubt, without a questioning mind, you will never find the happiness we all seek.

Thirdly, you need determination — a determination to keep searching for answers until all doubt is gone from your mind, a determination to find the answers to every question your mind can create.

If you have these three essentials, you will make swift progress.

Whether you are new to Celtic studies or widely read on the subject, this work is designed to provide a fresh perspective that will provoke thought and inspire positive change in every reader, regardless of background or belief. Through my own studies I have a peace and harmony in my life that I thought was just an impossible dream. I now walk this path every moment of every day and, if you can understand the world the way I do, you will understand the secret to happiness, health and fulfilment that is my daily reality.

As a Celt, I hold on to nothing and reject nothing. I have total freedom to look at faiths and beliefs and to extract the truth from all of them. With this in mind, I leave you with the words of a man who, I'm sure, would have seen much in common between his own teachings and those of the Celts.

Believe nothing, O monks, merely because you have been told it ... or because it is traditional, or because you yourselves have imagined it. Do not believe what your teacher tells you merely out of respect for the teacher. But whatsoever, after due examination and analysis, you find to be conducive to the good, the benefit, the welfare of all beings — that doctrine believe and cling to, and take it as your guide.

Buddha
(563–483 BCE)
The Dhammapada

One

THE SPIRAL OF LIFE

Wherever you look in the Celtic lands, you see circles and spirals. From the pre-Celtic stone circles and barrows to the wonderfully intricate Celtic knotwork used to decorate such things as weapons, jewellery and writing, our ancestors held circles and spirals as powerful and important images. The Druids committed very little to writing because they understood the power of words and felt that the written word was open to misinterpretation. Their language was one of symbols and both the circle and spiral were of great significance to them. They utilised stone circles as centres of ritual and also performed many of their ceremonies in the middle of circular groves of trees. Once you understand the power and influence of the many cycles in Nature upon humans, you begin to understand why circles, wheels and spirals were so important in the Celtic spiritual tradition. To understand how our ancestors perceived the world around them we must look at, and understand, creation ourselves.

Everything in creation is cyclical. Everything has a beginning, a middle and an end. We are born, we live and then we die, only to be reborn again on another plane of existence. Everywhere we look in Nature we see the cycle of birth, life, death and rebirth. In Nature nothing is ever still, its energies continue to move and evolve second by second, day after day, year after year. We know that even in the middle of winter there is life under the ground gathering its energies together in readiness for spring. Winter is always followed by spring, as death is followed by rebirth in a perpetual spiral of life. We also see the energies of birth, life and death in each passing day and yet we do not perceive their true power to teach us.

Everything in the universe is forever changing because the whole of creation is composed of energy in a permanently moving and changing state. Even solid objects are just collections of atoms and molecules in a state of constant movement on a planet that is spinning both on its own axis and around the sun. The solar system we inhabit is constantly moving and changing. Billions of years ago it was born and in billions of years it will die and its energy will form a new part of creation. Everywhere we look we perceive change, and yet change is the one thing we as modern, 'civilised' humans, resist.

We waste so much of our energy because we lack an understanding of our place within this wonderful universe we inhabit. We try to find stability in our lives, something tangible to believe in and fix our minds on, something to hold on to. If you understand the nature of the universe with its continual movement and change, then you will understand the futility of trying to hold on to things and the futility of resisting change. To understand the nature of the universe does not take years of study at university, it does not take a high IQ, indeed it is not dependent upon anything except your own ability to think. A small child understands the nature of the universe much better than you or me. Sadly, as it grows up, it is usually taught to abandon its understanding and embrace a new understanding, that of modern man. It is no coincidence that most small children are healthy and well, whereas adults are often unhealthy in mind and body. How you perceive and understand the universe has great bearing on your health and well-being overall. Everything is part of creation and has within it the spark of the creator. To understand the nature of the universe you need do no more than observe the wonders of creation around you. Mother Nature is full of deep wisdoms and profound teachings for which she will charge us nothing if we are only willing to open our minds to her.

Many people believe that complex thinking is advanced thinking, but the complete opposite is true. Take computers, for instance. With computers you can do millions of different things, from making music to running multi-million-dollar businesses. One computer can perform thousands of different tasks, from telling the time and date to transferring information around the world, and they have developed such diversity of function that much of our modern living is now dependent upon computers. They run hospitals, communications, banking, even traffic lights. What most people do not realise is that even the most complex computer is no more than a collection of switches that are either turned on or off. Computers use *binary code* to transfer information and this code is made up of a combination of zeros and ones. The zero turns a switch off and the one turns it on. If you take any computer to pieces you will find ultimately that it is composed of little more than simple, albeit minute, on/off switches housed in a plastic or metal box.

Complex thinking is not advanced thinking. It is futile thinking that wastes our energy and causes us illness. If we learn to think simply our lives will be simple. The next time you find yourself in a park or on a beach, take time to look at the little children at play and watch how they behave. See how they interact with the energies of people, animals, plants, stones and sand. The child lives in the present without fear or thought of the future or concern about the past. The balanced child holds on to nothing and rejects nothing. It plays with toys when they are available and, when they are not, it quickly turns its attention to something else and uses the power of its imagination to stimulate its mind.

To fully understand the universe, we need to think as children. We need to learn to let go of the past and live in the present. All thoughts of regret are a waste of energy because the past cannot be changed; any thoughts about behaving differently in the past are pointless. The only purpose the past serves is to teach and instruct us. We should not look at the past with regret but with open eyes eager to understand the lessons life has to teach us, whilst embracing the beauty that is today. If you spend all your time dwelling on the past, you have no power in the present. Similarly, if you spend all your time pondering potential future scenarios you will achieve very little with your life. The future is unwritten and, however you picture it, it will never be exactly the way you thought. How much time have you spent endlessly imagining the future, only to find the reality very different?

Our ancestors lived very much in the present although this does not mean that their thoughts never went beyond the day they were living. They knew that to survive the winter, they needed to hunt and gather food in the autumn, but they also knew that, however much they prepared, they could not foresee every future difficulty. Our ancestors survived because they expected the unexpected. They understood that the future is unwritten. They also understood the cycles of the land and so were in a much stronger position to predict how events were most likely to unfold.

The Celtic Wheel

The moon, seasons, planets, stars, comets and eclipses all have an effect on us and all have a cyclic nature. The Celts observed this and used a symbol to represent this. That symbol was a circle. They also divided the circle in various ways to punctuate it and so mark the passage of time. The circle was divided into four (reflecting the seasons, the elements, the cardinal directions), eight (the eight fire festivals) or thirteen (the thirteen tree months), all of which are discussed in some detail in later chapters. The Celtic Wheel is a map that allows one to see clearly where one is in life and what the future is most likely to hold. It shows the beginning, the middle and the end of the cycles of creation and so acts as a guide for the journey through life.

Imagine you have a problem for which you can see no solution. Which of the following scenarios would you prefer?

You spend all day and night pondering the problem with no success. The next two days are the same but after three days of hard thinking combined with little food or sleep you suddenly see the solution.

You see that it is the beginning of the Dark Moon phase and recognise that a solution is unlikely to manifest until the New Moon arrives. Bearing this in mind, you carry on life as normal safe in the knowledge

that the New Moon will bring with it new perspectives. Three days
later the solution suddenly pops into your head.

If life were really like that, the second scenario seems much less
painful. Well, life is like that if you choose to see it that way.
Everything in life is connected to everything else. The wheels of
creation that whirl around us affect us on a yearly, monthly, weekly,
daily and hourly basis. The Celtic Wheel maps out these cycles
and shows you exactly where you are on the map and thus where
you are in any unfolding process. Once you learn to flow with the
Wheel, you can make swift and sure progress on your spiritual
journey through life, but try to resist its turning and the Wheel will
knock you down again and again. Trying to stop the Wheel of Life
from turning is like trying to stop the sun from rising.

Life is full of problems but any problem is only a problem
because of how we perceive it. Once you view a problem from a
different perspective, you are much more likely to find a solution.
In fact a solution is no more than a problem viewed from a new
perspective. The Celtic Wheel provides us with just that: a new
perspective from which to view life and the challenges it brings
— one that will help us understand the interconnectedness of
everything in creation.

The power of the sun

Without the sun, there would be no life on this planet. We depend
upon its energies for our very existence. It is the source of all life
as we know it and we measure the passage of time by its rising
and setting, much as our ancestors did. Every time the sun rises,
the miracle of life is illuminated for all to see. If you suffer from
depression, try getting out of bed and watching the sunrise each
morning; it is very hard to be depressed after seeing such a
miracle. The rising sun brings new hope and a new beginning
each and every day. How often do people wait to view things 'in
the light of day'? This is because we subconsciously know the sun
illuminates the mind, but we have lost our conscious awareness
of its power and wisdom.

Every new day is a new beginning. The past is gone and the future unwritten, which means that every day is an opportunity for a fresh start. Every new dawn is like a blank piece of paper on which you can write your destiny. You have the power each morning to create your own reality, to set forth your dream and choose your destiny. We all have this power and yet we seldom use it. Instead, we would rather drag into each new day the emotional baggage from previous days, or even years, and as we do so we wonder why we are always so tired. On the road of life, the man who travels light makes the swiftest progress. Our Celtic ancestors understood this, but our modern greed and need to accumulate material wealth has taken us away from this true path of enlightenment and self-improvement.

Each dawn you create your own reality. You choose whether or not to get out of bed, what to wear, what to eat, and so on. You also choose what occupies your mind. If you wake up angry it is because you are subconsciously choosing to hold on to anger. No one can make you angry, the same as no one can make you sad. These are emotions that come from within, not without. The Celts believed that every individual is totally responsible for everything that manifests into their life. This does not mean that you are to blame for everything. Blame is an emotion we attach to events from which we feel we have nothing to learn or from which we do not wish to learn. What it means is that if something manifests into your life, you have drawn it in with your energy in order to learn. In any given situation you always have a choice about how you respond and how you perceive things. There is always more than one way to respond and more than one way to see things. Many people view life as a game of chance with people as pawns of fate, but that is only one view. The Celtic perspective offers a more productive and proactive view of life.

Everything that happens to you is an opportunity for you to grow in strength and wisdom. So often we view things as 'bad' because we do not perceive that they are just part of an unfolding cycle. If you suffer a hardship that challenges you to dig deep within yourself and tap into previously undiscovered inner strengths or that teaches you something new about yourself or the world you inhabit, the hardship may appear bad but the outcome of the process can be very good. It is how you respond to the challenges that life presents to you that determines whether something is good or bad.

How you think, how you perceive life, is entirely up to you. To me, life is full of magic, and the human mind is one of the most magical things in creation. The power to imagine and create dreams allows us the freedom to go anywhere and do anything. If you put out a pure intent, you will attract to you all the energies that are needed to make that intent reality. For instance, you may put out the intent to be a healer. If your intent is pure and does not come from the ego, you will begin to attract into your life the lessons that are required to make that dream reality. The problem many people have is that they put out such intents but then complain when their lessons manifest. They expect to get an easy road and often fall at the first obstacle. If you want the life of your dreams then you have to be willing to work for it. You can do anything you desire if you have enough hunger for it; obstacles only manifest into our lives to be overcome and to make us wiser and stronger.

The nature of cycles

All cycles have a beginning (birth), a middle (growth) and an end (death). Beginnings, like births, are always challenging. When a baby is born it has to learn millions of lessons in its first few months of life. It has to learn to sit up, crawl, then walk and it has to learn to communicate effectively. All beginnings are the same. Whenever you start any process or cycle of learning, the steepest part of the learning curve comes in the initial stages. As the process unfolds, like the growth through childhood, you gain a greater understanding of the process and tend to flow with it. The problem is that we as modern humans have a fear of death. This means that we often tend to get stuck in the middle of things rather than bringing our learning processes to completion in order to allow ourselves to initiate a new process.

How many people, when they reach adulthood, still hanker after the carefree life of a child? Adulthood means the death of childhood. This does not mean that you lose your childhood, but it does mean you let go of it. This allows your mind the freedom to progress and expand its knowledge whilst also having the freedom to walk among childhood memories and childlike attitudes without detriment. Death is not a bad thing, it is just a process of letting go. Every time you go to sleep at night, it is like a death process. You have the opportunity to let go of all cares and worries from the past and allow yourself peaceful rest and rejuvenation ready for the birth of a new day. If you feel that you cannot let go of your worries, take them out of your mind and put them in a box or drawer beside your bed each night. You can then take them back in the morning if you wish. This may sound a bit strange, but it does work. If you imagine putting negative thoughts away for the night in a drawer, it creates a message for the mind to let go of them without the ego feeling threatened.

Every day is a cycle of life and death, embracing and letting go. Everything in life comes to teach and, the more we dislike something in our lives, the more it has to teach us. If you fight a problem you compound it by giving it your power and energy. But if you embrace a problem with pleasure and learn from it you will draw power and energy from it until a solution manifests. This is the way of the universe; this is the spiral of life. If you learn to walk the spiral, rather than remaining static and comfortable, your quality of life and inner peace will improve day by day.

It is a mistake to seek a comfortable life. Countries such as Canada and Sweden have a very high standard of living combined with low unemployment. The vast majority of the people living in these countries have a comfortable life and yet the suicide rate in both is amongst the highest in the world. Being comfortable is not healthy and it does not bring happiness, only stagnation. The person who has an easy life learns very little and is unfulfilled. The person who has a hard life but who learns from all of his or her experiences becomes wise and with that wisdom finds happiness, health and fulfilment. You should never be satisfied with where you are in life. This does not mean that you should be forever dissatisfied. What it means is that no matter what your life is like at the moment, you have more to learn and with that learning comes improvement in the quality of your life.

Every day can, and should, be an adventure full of surprises and insights if you learn to flow in harmony with the energies of creation. So often we miss opportunities for personal growth and deeper understanding because we fail to see our lessons. Our minds are so full of worries and irrelevant thoughts that there is no space to perceive our lessons as they come to us. Everything is significant and we can learn from any and every situation if our minds are not filled with irrelevant thoughts. *Think simply and simply think* — there is always a simple solution to any problem and, if you cannot find it, it is because your thinking is too complex.

The power of the moon

Perhaps the most powerful and influential cycle is that of the moon. Our ancestors knew this and planned much of their lives around the moon, from planting and harvesting to marriage and magic. Since ancient times it has been recognised that the moon has great influence upon the mind. The root word for 'moon', 'mind' and 'mania' is the same; and 'lunar' and 'lunacy' share a common origin. The original meaning of 'lunacy' was 'moon-struck' and it was a word conjured up by the Christians to try to deter worship of the moon goddess Luna. It is also an established fact that the incidence of suicides and admissions to mental institutions is always greatest around the Full Moon. Animals and children become more active and excitable around the Full Moon — and so do you, although you may not be consciously aware of it. Next time you are having a difficult day or things just don't seem to be running as smoothly as normal, look at where the moon is in its cycle. Often these situations arise on or around the Dark and the Full Moon. Once you understand this you can be better prepared for such times and will understand better how to handle them.

Approximately every twenty-eight days the moon goes through its cycle of waxing and waning. It changes its appearance in the sky over this time and these changes are marked by four main phases. The New Moon marks the first illumination when no more than a sliver of light is visible in the night sky. The moon then 'grows' or waxes until the First Quarter when half of the disc of the moon is visible. It continues to wax until a full circle of light is visible in the sky — the Full Moon. It then begins to wane, decreasing in size to the Third Quarter when again only half a disc is visible and continues until the disc is not visible at all. This fifth phase, the Dark Moon, lasts for three nights and is the most powerful of all times of the month.

The New Moon always marks a time of new beginnings and positive change. It marks the dawn of each lunar month and like the dawning of the sun, it is a blank piece of paper on which we write our future. As the moon grows in power, so too does its influence on the world and this is greatest at Full Moon. The energies of the earth are at their most agitated at this time and it can be very challenging to remain balanced and centred in the days leading up to and after the Full Moon. Both the New and the Full Moon mark nodal points in the cycle of creation that unfolds each month in the world around and within us. This is especially true in plants, humans and animals, We are all made up mostly of water and the moon's influence over the rise and fall of fluids on the earth affects not only the tides, but also our internal fluids. When we are presented with any challenge or difficulty in life, observation of the moon shows us that movement forward invariably coincides with either the New Moon or the Full Moon when there is an internal change in the flow of our bodily fluids. This is because the change of flow affects fluids flowing to and from the brain and, when the internal chemistry of the brain changes, so too does our perception of reality. As these perceptions change, our perspective changes and hence we find new ways to proceed.

The moon, with its cycle of birth, growth and death, is a strong reminder each month of the nature of cycles. At one time all women's menstrual cycles were in perfect harmony with the moon. A woman would ovulate on the Full Moon and menstruate on the Dark Moon. The Full Moon is the culmination of the cycle of creation, when the egg is finally released. In the fourteen days prior to this release, the energies of creation gather together all the things needed to make the egg. Once the Full Moon has passed, if the egg has not been fertilised, it begins to become overripe until it decays, dies and is shed in the natural flow of blood at the Dark Moon. Furthermore, if a woman eats and lives in harmony with the land, she only bleeds for the three days of the Dark Moon. When the New Moon emerges, her flow naturally stops and the cycle of creation begins again within her.

In our modern society, full of chemicals and contraceptive pills, it is harder for women to embody and understand this cycle of creation and destruction within themselves and even harder for men to understand. We have become so fearful of death that we dare not seek the power of the Dark Moon, the most potent of all the moon's phases, in our lives. But without death there would be no life and every cycle we go through involves death as much as it does life. Death is a dark doorway of opportunity that, if we learn to step through it without fear, will always lead us into the light of new understandings and realisations.

Our Celtic ancestors ran their lives in harmony with the cycles of both sun and moon. They honoured the rising sun each morning, acknowledging its power and influence, and they honoured its sister, the moon. The link between women and the moon was utilised by the Celts in their approach to planting and harvesting crops. The decision about when to sow seeds was always governed by women because they were regarded as embodying creation each month in their menstrual cycle. It followed that if a woman embodied both life and death, she would best know the correct time for the creation of life in the fields. In those times women were so in touch with their own bodies and intuition that they knew with certainty the very best times to sow and harvest. This is a resource lost to most modern women but one they can reclaim if they once again live in harmony with the land.

To the Celts, all the different cycles and phenomena in Nature were perceived to have strong influences upon mankind. Comets, eclipses and other unusual events were seen as omens foretelling times of upheaval and change. It was the way of the universe and the Celts understood that, the more they observed and studied the heavens and earth, the more they would understand their own place within the web of life. The Celtic ability to embrace change was largely due to the fact that they had no concept of ownership like we do today. They believed that everything we possess is merely borrowed and that, when it is time for things to leave us, trying to fight the process only makes it painful. This allowed the Celts to embrace change with pleasure and walk onwards in their lives without regret. Whether they had to let go of their negative emotions, physical possessions or loved ones, they did so without fear or pain.

Their approach to possessions, though, did not mean that anyone could come and steal their land. The Celts were ferocious warriors and, to protect their sacred lands from those who might not treat the land with respect, would fight to the death. This was not out of possessiveness, but out of honour. The Celts regarded themselves as guardians of the land and of all the plants, rocks and creatures that lived upon it. They took their guardianship very seriously recognising that their own survival depended upon it. It was this attitude that meant that the Celts were admired by all who met them.

What made the Celts especially feared by their opponents in battle was their lack of any fear of death. They believed that the journey of the soul spans many lifetimes and that the death of one life means rebirth into another. From the Celtic perspective, the life you are now experiencing is just one of many lives over many years that make up the journey of your soul. Your soul is the spiritual part of you that survives death and is sometimes referred to as your 'higher self'. When a soul is not within a human body, it is in 'spirit', a state of existence where concepts of space and time no longer exist. The human form provides the soul with a vehicle through which it can learn and experience many things on many levels. Life is a school of learning and you have a choice as to whether you embrace life's lessons and become wiser and stronger or ignore such things and learn little.

Everything you experience in life is an opportunity to learn. Things only appear 'bad' or negative to us because we have failed to understand what we are meant to learn from them. To the Celts, our approach to life would have seemed very strange. We give our power away to so many things. We look to food to make us feel better when true happiness only comes from within. Similarly, our happiness is often dependent upon other people behaving in the ways we want them to. If they do things that hurt us, our happiness is shattered. We have lost sight of true happiness. True happiness comes only from within and is not dependent upon others. When we learn to live in harmony with creation around us, as I believe the Celts did, we find the joy and satisfaction in life that we are all seeking.

We are living in one of the most exciting times in this planet's long and turbulent history. The past millennium has been one ruled by men and the time is now dawning for the balance to be redressed. This does not mean that women will gain the ascendancy, but that the dawn of a new era of understanding and mutual respect between men and women is upon us. Just as our lives run in cycles, so too does the life of this planet. Grandmother Earth is about to die and be reborn. The prophecies about the end of the earth predict not only death, but also rebirth. Our society, run on materialism and greed, is about to break down because our planet will not tolerate us being so out of balance with her. Just as our bodies repel the invasion of micro-organisms that could harm us, so too will the earth repel those who rape and abuse her. Evolution has taught us that in order to survive one must learn to adapt. As the earth rebalances herself to clear away the toxic waste that we have poisoned her with over the past two centuries, only those that work with her will understand how to survive the metamorphosis.

The Celtic Otherworld

The Celts did not have a concept of heaven like most other religions. They believed in an Otherworld that was as rich and diverse as the world we inhabit. It had regions, islands, forests and caves that were inhabited by gods, fairies, supernatural animals and other magical beings. It existed in the same space as this world but in another dimension and could be crossed into in many different ways. Sacred hills, mounds, lakes, rivers, mists and forests all contained doorways to this world and travel to it was so easy that many Celtic heroes were not even aware that they had 'crossed over'. Otherworldly beings could also gain access to this world and often did so to bring help or teaching to ordinary folk.

The *Underworld*, or **Annwn**, the land of the dead, was part of the Otherworld but was not seen as a place of darkness and fear. On the contrary, the whole of the Otherworld was a realm of beauty, harmony and magic where the dead would continue their existence and sometimes return resurrected to the physical world. It could also be accessed through dreams and visions and was a place where the normal rules of this world did not apply. Animals could talk and humans could change form in order to experience different states of existence for insight and understanding.

To the Celts the Otherworld was as real as this world and shamans would often be described as living in both worlds. I too believe in the Otherworld and have witnessed some of its magic in my life. The fact that we no longer acknowledge its existence in modern society is due to the restrictive influence both of science and the Church. We have sadly lost our faith in the power of magic in our lives by becoming obsessed with trying to hold on to possessions and with the accumulation of wealth. The Christian concepts of hell and damnation are a tactic designed to instil fear in spiritual exploration and to create conformity of behaviour, but, as modern society shows, ruling by fear creates resentment, rebellion and ill health. We have lost our sense of personal responsibility for the health of our bodies and souls and, with it, our inheritance of a life of magic and wonder.

The modern attitude to spirituality is just that — an attitude — and attitudes can be changed with the speed of thought. If you do not believe in magic, your lack of belief prevents you from experiencing it in your life. If, however, you open your mind to

THE SPIRAL OF LIFE

the limitless possibilities of this wonderful universe you will experience magic in the rising of each sun, in the beauty of creation and in your day-to-day life. This might seem like fantasy but, to me, it is reality. I choose to believe in the possibility of a magical world and so I see magic in everything. I believe it is possible to communicate with all of creation and so I have magical encounters with trees, plants, animals and stones that give me new insights and understandings about myself and my purpose as a spiritual being.

On more than one occasion I have been told that I live in a 'fantasy world', but this fantasy world has enabled me to find happiness, health and fulfilment in my life and to show many people how to achieve the same. Other people view it as fantasy because their own minds are closed to the possibility of magic in their lives. To say 'I don't believe in magic' is to create a self-limiting philosophy that prevents you from finding true happiness, health and fulfilment. Whether you choose to believe me or not makes no difference to *my* life because *your* happiness, health and fulfilment do not depend upon acceptance by me or anyone else, they depend only upon acceptance by you.

There is a tale that clearly demonstrates how to live life. One day a magician was out walking with his young apprentice in the mountains collecting rare herbs. It was the first time the young boy had seen the mountains and he was unfamiliar with the dangers of rocky places. Running on ahead he suddenly tripped and fell very heavily. 'Ahhh!' he shouted in pain and to his amazement a voice from within the mountains repeated, 'Ahhh!' 'Who's there?' the boy shouted. 'Who's there?' came the reply. 'Show yourself, you coward,' shouted the boy, growing angry, to which the voice said, 'Show yourself, you coward.' 'You are the most stupid and ignorant human being I have ever met,' he screamed, only to be met by the very same words. By this time the magician had arrived and the boy asked of him, 'What magic is this?'

The magician smiled and said, 'Listen carefully, my boy. Men call this magic an echo but it is really the wise god of the mountains who teaches us the simplest rule of life. 'You're beautiful,' shouted the magician. 'You're beautiful,' came the reply. 'I love you,' shouted the magician. 'I love you,' responded the echo. 'You see,' the magician quietly told the boy, 'life is what you put into it. If you think only beautiful thoughts, speak only beautiful words, do only beautiful things, then your life will be rewarded with beauty in return. If you let lies, deceit and selfishness be your allies, then you will be living in a world of illusion, never needing to fear hell because you will already be living it.'

Two

THE FOUR ELEMENTS

The four elements, Earth, Air, Fire and Water, form the basic structure of the Celtic Medicine Wheel. They represent the universe from microcosm to macrocosm; everything that exists is an embodiment of the four elements. The Celtic concept of creation, like that of the ancient Egyptians, is that 'God' created the universe from his own being — God the Creator is the union of the four elements in perfect harmony from whom all life derives. We are created from the four elements and it is our path, if we choose it, to learn how to hold the four elements in perfect harmony.

The four elements are representations of patterns of energy and should not be confused with physical earth, air, fire and water. As we learn to balance the elements, or energies, we grow in spiritual wisdom and thus find our true connection with the divine.

There is a fifth element, Ether. Ether is the ethereal, the spiritual. Ether is that place of balance and harmony that we are all seeking. It is the connection to the wisdom of the universe that will allow us, once we have found it within ourselves, to fulfil our true destinies as spiritual beings in a spiritual universe.

To understand the four elements is to understand yourself. Once you understand them, you will see them in everything you look at, feel them in everything you touch and sense them with every thought. If you learn how to find that place of balance within yourself, you will find true happiness, health and freedom.

Nature shows us very clearly how to achieve balance. She turns on a perpetual wheel of birth, growth, death and rebirth. She embodies the four elements in dynamic equilibrium and, if left alone by man, she will always find balance and harmony.

The Celtic view of the universe is multi-dimensional. The Celts understood that the universe exists on many different levels and that life can be viewed in many different ways. Take yourself, for instance. You can view yourself as a tiny insignificant dot in an ever-expanding universe or you can view yourself as a whole universe. It is all a matter of perspective. You can view yourself in countless ways and the four elements can be viewed in just as many.

Like everything in the Celtic world, the four elements are beautifully simple, yet infinitely complex. They are metaphors that can allow us to understand the world around and within us more deeply. It is by truly understanding the simple that you will be able to fully understand the complex. Once you understand a simple truth on one level, it can be applied to any thing at any level.

So, let us look in detail at the four elements. Each element has its own characteristics and these can be applied to everything in creation.

The four elements and the natural world

Earth embodies the energy of winter. It is the night-time, when darkness falls upon the earth. It is the North, the place from where the sun never shines, and so is naturally associated with a colder climate. The energy of Earth moves downwards and is cold. We see this movement and character in winter in the cold weather, in the many animals that sleep until spring and at night-time, the coldest time of the day, when we lie down to sleep. Earth is linked to the dark phase of the moon and is represented by the colour black, the colour of night, the colour of darkness.

Air embodies the energy of spring when plants draw up nutrients from the ground to feed their new growth. It is the morning, when we draw in the first energies of the rising sun and is linked to the East and to warmth. It has an inward energy, a sense of drawing in energy from outside, in the same way that we draw air into our lungs. It is the moon at its First Quarter and its colour is yellow, the colour of the morning sun.

Fire embodies the energies of summer and noon, the times when the power of the sun is at its strongest. It is the South and has a hot, expressive energy — when a fire starts it spreads in all directions. In the heat of the sun, at the height of the day, Nature is at its most active and expressive. Fire is also linked to the Full Moon when the light of the moon is at its brightest. Its colour is white, the colour of the sun at the height of a hot summer's day.

Water embodies the energy of autumn when the fruits are plump and full. It is the West, the direction of the setting sun, the evening. It has a cool, upward, buoyant energy and can be likened to the way we feel at the end of a hard but satisfying day's work. It is linked to the moon's Third Quarter and its colour is red, the colour of the setting sun.

The following table summarises the aspects of the four elements.

	Earth	Air	Fire	Water
Temperature	Cold	Warm	Hot	Cool
Direction	North	East	South	West
Season	Winter	Spring	Summer	Autumn
Lunar phase	Dark	First Quarter	Full	Third Quarter
Movement	Down	Inwards	Outwards	Up
Time of day	Night	Morning	Noon	Evening
Colour	Black	Yellow	White	Red

The elements and the human body

We can think of health and well-being in terms of the four elements. The human body has four aspects — structure, biochemistry, energy and the mind. Earth relates to the structure of the body and is linked with the physical body and sensation. Water relates to the biochemistry of the body and is linked to the emotions and feeling. Fire relates to the energy of the body and is linked with our energy pathways (acupuncture meridians) and intuition. Air relates to the mind, the place where all illness begins and where all cures can be found, and is linked with thinking and learning.

Therapies can also be thought of in terms of the four elements. Earth governs the physical therapies such as massage, reflexology, manipulation and bone-setting. Air governs counselling and other mind-therapies. Fire governs therapies that build and move energy, such as healing, crystal-healing and acupuncture. Water governs therapies like nutrition and herbs that act directly on the body's biochemistry. In Celtic times the therapies most likely practised by the shaman would include massage, manipulation, bone-setting, counselling, healing, nutrition and herbs. The Celtic warriors also practised martial arts and wilderness survival skills, which would have improved the quality of all four elements within them, thus improving physical strength, mental acuity, energy levels and biochemical power.

Each element has related organs and character types. The kidneys belong to Earth. The kidneys keep our energy grounded and power our determination. People with strong kidney energies are fearless and enjoy hard work. They are often thought of as 'down to earth' and are good at getting 'down' to tasks. They have strong bones and are often physically very active. These sorts of people thrive on stress and enjoy pushing themselves to the limit. The bladder is also an Earth organ because of the downward movement of urine out of the body and into the earth. Strange as it may seem, the action of passing urine helps to ground you. Sometimes, especially in children, when fear rises in the body, the bladder tries to help ground the individual by releasing urine, which is why fearful situations can sometimes lead to people wetting themselves. It is simply the body trying to restore balance.

The lungs naturally are linked to the element of Air. Just as we draw air into our lungs to breathe, so we draw energies and lessons to us in order to improve our minds. Air is linked to learning and our best learning comes through social interaction. (We will talk more about the process of learning through social interaction later.) People with strong lung energy are usually very social, thriving upon discussion and debate. They seek to draw resources to themselves in order to learn and are often left-brain dominant.

We have two main sections in the brain, the left brain and the right brain. The left brain controls logical thinking. It works in a logical, step-by-step manner with one thought leading on to the next. The right brain controls our intuition and expression. It works in a more random manner linking seemingly unrelated thoughts together to allow us to make new connections. It is the part of us that sees the big picture and has the power of true objectivity. One side of the brain often appears more dominant in different individuals. Left-brain-dominant people cannot see the big picture like right-brain people can but, once they are shown it, they can see all the steps that need to be taken to make that vision reality.

The large intestine or colon is also linked to Air. This is because it is the organ where waste matter is compacted, which is an inward energy. Some people equate the colon with downward energy because of the downward motion in defecation, but this happens in the rectum, not the colon. The colon is a long tube that travels up the right side of the body, across under the bottom of the rib cage and down the left side of the body before making its final descent to the rectum. During its journey through the colon, food is compacted, hence its link to Air. It may seem perverse to be discussing the excretory functions of the body but these functions are as important to our health and well-being as any other function. Many westerners are embarrassed to discuss such matters but examination of the quality of urine and faeces can give you a great deal of valuable information about how your body is functioning.

The liver is linked to the element of Fire and is the organ in charge of the free-flow of energy and nutrients around the body. People with strong liver energies are very expressive. They often have a strong sense of destiny, which is how we express our lives. They tend to do a lot of work on themselves in terms of personal development because they understand that it is only through improving your own levels of personal power that you can make your destiny a living reality. They tend to be right-brain dominant with visionary and intuitive characteristics.

The reason intuition is linked to Fire, an expressive energy, is because when we use our powers of intuition we tap into higher realms of consciousness. This 'tapping in' is an expressive movement of the energy of the mind. This confuses some people because they equate psychic powers with intuition and think of people with psychic abilities as tending to draw psychic energies to themselves, which is more like the energy movement of Air than Fire. True, intuition is a psychic power but it is only one of many different types of spiritual energies that we can utilise on our spiritual path, and not all are linked to Air. Psychic gifts such as clairvoyance do rely upon the practitioner drawing energy inwards, but the intuition works in the opposite way and is used to judge the truth of information received in this manner.

The gall bladder, an organ that rests on the underside of the liver is also linked to Fire as it expresses bile (that it has collected from the liver) into the small intestine to help with digestion.

The heart is linked to the energy of Water and with the ebb and flow of emotions it produces. It is connected to nurturing and nourishment, rest and relaxation. People with strong heart energies are naturally loving and giving. They lift people's spirits with their bubbly energy and are always good to have around when you are feeling low. They love cooking and make the perfect hosts. They move their own energies and the energies of those around them upward by embodying the buoyant nature of Water.

The small intestine is also linked to Water because of its role in the body's nourishment through digestion. It is the place into which bile from the gall bladder and pancreatic juices flow to aid the body's digestion.

The spleen and pancreas are linked to the fifth element, Ether. These organs are central to the balance within the body as they are connected to the production and maintenance of the blood. Ether also governs the function of the stomach, the organ that energises the spleen and pancreas.

Ether signifies the place where all of the other elements are held in balance. This point of balance needs to be found on every level of our beings before we can find true peace and happiness.

These levels are the physical (Earth), emotional (Water), destiny (Fire), mental (Air) and spiritual (Ether).

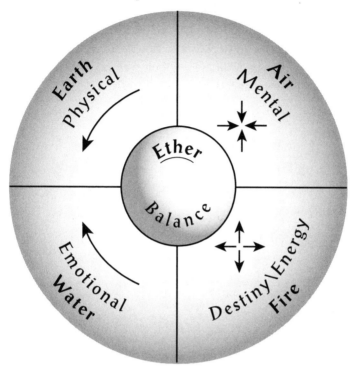

The ingredients of true balance, peace and harmony

There are also wheels within wheels. For example, on a physical level, this balance (Ether) means we should have a time to work (Earth), a time to rest (Water), a time for self (Fire) and a time for social interaction (Air). At each level, each one of which is linked to an element, you can find the elements working together within that level.

Illness manifests due to an imbalance between two or more elements. For example, we know that people who work too much and don't rest enough often have heart attacks. This is caused by an Earth–Water imbalance. They neglect the Water element and thus weaken their hearts. Similarly, people who spend all their time giving to other people at the expense of their own well-being become weak and disempowered. They overwork their Water element and thus lose the power of Earth in their lives. People with mental problems (Air weakness) tend to cut themselves off from society (remember that Air is connected with learning through social interaction) and people who don't express themselves and use addictions to try to hide from their own pain often have liver problems (Fire weakness).

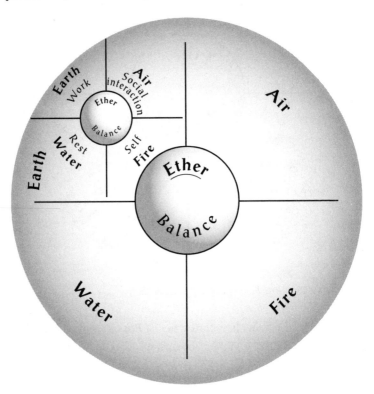

Balancing the elements within the elements

There are also links between each element and the openings in the body. Earth relates to the lower orifices because the body excretes downwards. (The inner ear is also linked to the kidneys and, thus, the Earth element: dizziness and vertigo are caused by Earth weakness when the kidneys are too weak to hold down the body's energy and consequently excess energy rises to the head.

These energy surges affect the inner ear causing the symptoms of ungroundedness (dizziness) and so, without the correct functioning of the inner ear, one cannot remain grounded.)

Air relates to the nose, the organ that filters the air that we breathe into our lungs. Fire relates to the eyes. This is because Fire is linked to the right brain which is the visionary part of us. Water is linked to the ears and hearing. Do you notice how animals and humans all move upwards when trying to hear something faint? They 'prick up their ears' mirroring the upward energy movement of Water.

Ether relates to the mouth because what enters through our mouths dictates the health of the spleen and pancreas and therefore affects our overall inner balance. Ether also has a link to the sinuses. They clean the blood before it enters the brain. If the blood entering the brain is not clean because of poor sinuses, both the left and right brain become imbalanced and this stops us making connections to the higher realms of consciousness from where we find balance. Inflamed sinuses are an Ether weakness due to too many toxins in the blood and, when this occurs, all the other elements and their related organs are affected.

The elements also govern the tissues within the body. Earth governs the bones (structure); Air, the skin (we actually breathe through our skin as well as our lungs); Fire, the muscles and tendons (vital for physical expression); Water, the circulatory system and blood vessels; and Ether, the blood and flesh in which is carried the energy of life and creation.

The elements and the emotions

Each element is linked to an emotion. The emotion linked to Earth is fear. Fear is caused by a lack of grounding and power. It manifests as energy rising up in the body. When in a fearful situation, a person with weak Earth energies feels powerless. Their shoulders rise up and their breathing becomes restricted. This is clearly seen when someone has a panic attack. They lose the ability to ground their fear and it rises up in the body making the face sweat and causing mental imbalance. However, when someone with strong

Earth energy feels fear rising within them, they 'think' themselves grounded. They tap into their power and face the situation ready to fight or flee. This in turn activates another Earth organ, the adrenals.

Whenever we meet fearful situations, the adrenal glands, located upon the upper end of each kidney, secrete a substance called adrenaline. This stimulates the sympathetic nervous system within the body which in turn stimulates the heart to raise blood pressure, increases the amount of glucose in the blood and constricts the smaller blood vessels. Adrenaline also stops bleeding and opens up the breathing. All this prepares the body for high levels of potentially injurious physical activity — fighting or fleeing. When someone has weak Earth energy, they become gripped by fear and, because they are ungrounded, they have the ability neither to fight nor to flee.

All fears and phobias are manifestations of Earth energy weakness. Different levels of fear indicate different levels of weakness. People with very weak Earth energies live with fear most of the time. When the weakness becomes chronic they can show kidney weakness, lower back problems (due to kidney and adrenal fatigue), physical weakness and vertigo. All these symptoms point back to a single cause once you understand the elements. People with fear in their lives need to strengthen their Earth/kidney energy. Once they become more powerful and stronger, their fear will subside.

To strengthen Earth energy you need to do things that will increase your Earth connection and build up your strength. Connecting with Nature is one of the best grounding and energising things you can do. Just a simple walk in the park will improve your Earth energy and a walk in a forest or by the sea is even more powerful. Earth energy is also connected with determination, so setting yourself tasks of increasing difficulty with also improve its levels.

The emotion linked to Air is anxiety. To understand this link, we need to further understand the qualities of Air as an element. Air is all about resources. Resources are things we either possess or seek. The air we breathe is a vital resource (without it we die), but there are other resources in our lives, many of which we are not even aware of. Every skill you possess, everything you do is a potential resource for you. We are each born with a set of resources or 'talents'. During our journey through life, we seek to improve the quality of our resources and to discover new ones. We do this best through social interaction. Everyone we meet has something to teach us, a resource to give us, and we too have things to teach all the people we meet in our lives. Whenever we meet another person, a subconscious trade in resources takes place. Sometimes the trade is only one way if one of the parties chooses not to learn and, sometimes, no trade goes on at all! This is not through a lack of resources in each person but through a lack of understanding of the true purpose of life. Life is an unending opportunity to learn and grow if we choose to look inward and learn from everything that comes into our lives.

Sometimes you meet someone for the first time and feel strongly attracted to his or her energy. Often, after only a few minutes, you feel and act like old friends. This is because you both subconsciously recognise resources in each other to trade. The attraction is cemented by the energy exchanges that take place during conversation and these take place on many different levels — for example, physically, in body language (Earth); subconsciously or psychically (Air); verbally (Fire); emotionally (Water); and spiritually (Ether).

Anxiety is caused by a lack of resources. When viewed in this way, the solution is simple: go and find the resources you are lacking. For instance, if you are anxious about your driving test because you don't know how to reverse properly, the solution is to find someone who knows how to reverse properly and get them to teach you. In this situation, the resource you are lacking is knowledge of how to reverse correctly and the solution is to find someone who possesses that resource and who will share it with you.

Some resources are harder to locate though. Often people do not know what they are seeking, they are just anxious. This is because they do not understand what the emotion is trying to teach them. Everything comes into your life to teach you and anxiety is no different. The key to understanding the lessons of anxiety lies in looking within. It is only through introspection that one can find the resources needed to allay anxiety. Once these lacking resources are recognised, one naturally attracts someone with those resources into one's life. The problem is that people are so unused to thinking in this way that they miss many opportunities to learn. In truth, you possess all the resources you need within you. When other people 'teach' you, what they are really doing is showing you how to locate resources within yourself.

Ultimately, the answers to all your questions and the solutions to all your problems lie within you. The spiritual journey is a journey of self-discovery that helps you to uncover those hidden resources that lie dormant within you.

There is another emotional trait linked to Air: judging others. We can only gather resources if we are willing to learn. This means that Air is also about learning your lessons in life. When we judge other people, what we are really doing is diverting attention away from our own, unlearnt lessons. But we have no right to judge other people, only ourselves. Judging others comes about when we make assumptions about other people. For instance, imagine you meet someone at a party whom you haven't seen for a long time. You go up to them with a big smile on your face only to be greeted by a blank stare. Undeterred, you begin to reminisce with them about old times, but they seem totally disinterested in you and what you have to say. You finally lose patience and ask them why they are being so rude but they silently turn and walk away. If you judge them, you might think they were ignorant and un-caring. Imagine your horror if you discovered later, that they had only minutes before learnt about the death of a close family member and were still in state of shock when you greeted them. Who then might be the ignorant and uncaring one? People who think and act this way are often avoiding learning their own lessons. In its extreme, some people are very critical of others yet are totally unaware of their own negative behaviour towards other people. A person with good Air energy makes neither assumptions nor judgements.

Anxiety and judgement of others are both symptoms of a lack of Air energy. Other symptoms can include lung problems like bronchitis, asthma, coughs and colds, skin problems such as rashes, psoriasis and eczema, and large intestine disorders such as constipation or colitis. All of these symptoms indicate Air weakness and the solution always lies in looking within and learning more about yourself.

Any situation that manifests into your life, whether it is a difficulty or even an illness, comes to teach. Many people fight these situations but this just feeds in energy and compounds the problem. If you begin learning from a situation, you draw energy away from it and once you have learnt all you need to learn, it will cease to exist in your life. This is true of all trials, hardships and illnesses. Correct breathing also helps to relieve these emotions, especially anxiety. Anxious people always have shallow breathing and by learning correct, deep breathing through meditation, Tai Chi or Yoga, one can improve the amount of oxygen running through the brain, making learning easier and calming the mind. The breath of life is more important than even food and water to our survival and yet it is the one resource most westerners fail to fully utilise.

The emotion linked with Fire is anger. Anger begins with suppression or lack of movement in a person's life. They suppress so much that eventually it bursts out as rage. In truth, anger often has nothing to do with other people, only with the self. If someone makes you angry, it is a signpost to an unresolved issue within yourself. A good way to understand the process of anger is to think of it as 'pushing buttons'. When someone makes you angry, they push a button within you that makes you give your energy away to them. They have power over you because they evoke a response in you over which you have no control. If you become hurt and angry as a result of another's words, it is usually because there is truth within those words that you don't want to face. If someone said to you, 'You are an alien with green hair and no

arms,' you would not be upset. You would realise that they must
be either totally imbalanced or have a strange sense of humour to
perceive you in that way. However, if someone said to you, 'You
are deluding yourself if you think that you have respect for others,
because it is quite clear that you have no respect for yourself,' and
if there was a grain of truth in that statement, you may well get
angry with them. The anger would be a defence mechanism to
avert attention from the truth that you had just been faced with.
Sometimes we get angry when someone accuses us of being or
doing something that is totally untrue. This anger comes only
when the ego has not been mastered. If someone says things about
you that are untrue, it is often only your pride that is hurt. Once
the ego is mastered you realise that you never need to prove a
truth, only walk it. If you walk your truth every moment of every
day, your actions will speak louder than any words of defence.

Anger can also come from a lack of expression. If you are
dominated by another person, if someone uses their energy to
stop you doing the things you would like to do, then anger can
often rise within you. Still, the anger is nothing really to do with
the other person, but with you. If you want to be free from anger,
you have to learn how to express yourself by finding your destiny. Finding your destiny is what Fire is all about. People who
follow their true destiny are free from anger because they are
expressing their lives in the way that they want to.

Fire weakness often manifests as liver problems. People with
Fire weakness can also develop eye weakness, middle back pain,
vitamin and mineral deficiency, gallstones and high blood
pressure (from suppressing too much emotion within themselves).
The key to resolving all these problems lies in finding your
destiny. All Fire weakness is caused by a lack of expression and,
at its most fundamental level, this relates to not expressing our
lives in a healthy way. Everyone wants to be happy, healthy and
fulfilled. It is our destiny, should we choose to embrace it, to learn
from life and to find balance and harmony. This means that, if we
actively seek happiness, health and fulfilment in our lives, we will
naturally connect with our destiny because balance and harmony

mean 'happiness, health and fulfilment'. All forms of expression — art, music, poetry and dance, for example — improve one's Fire energy, as do energy-building exercises like Tai Chi and Chi Kung. I am sure that the Celts had their own martial arts and energy-building exercises but such knowledge has been lost with time so we look to the east for this teaching.

The emotion linked to Water is depression. Depression is a lack of joy and upliftedness. It is an unhealthy downward energy. The downward energy of the element Earth has a sense of 'rootedness' — it is your connection to the earth and relates primarily to the lower half of the body. But depression is downward heart/Water energy primarily relating to the upper half of the body. Phrases such as 'feeling a bit down' clearly show that we unconsciously recognise this energy movement. The kidneys connect us to the physical world and the heart connects us to the spiritual world via the emotions. Together they allow perfect balance of body, mind and spirit.

Depression is usually caused by one of two factors. Either the person has given out too much energy, or they are holding on to an energy that is not good for them. As we have already seen, Water people are loving and giving, but that loving and giving needs to exist in a balanced fashion. Some people 'give too much' and this is because they are seeking to make other people happy usually at the expense of their own happiness. Trying to make other people happy is a fruitless task. You truly only have the power to make yourself happy and it is the same for all people. If you want those you love to be happy, you have to teach them how. The only way you can do this is by finding happiness yourself.

The joy that comes from having balanced Water energy is a deep well of joy that cannot be taken away by anything or anyone. You should be able to find peace and happiness no matter what is going on in your life. You should be happy whether you are eating a banquet or a plain bowl of rice, whether you are feeling wonderful or are wracked with pain, whether you have just won the lottery or have just had your house repossessed. Depression comes from a lack of understanding of the true nature of the universe. *Nothing is good or bad in the world until humans interact with it.* Even if someone is really nasty towards you, it is neither a good nor a bad thing until you react to that energy. Your reaction can either weaken you or empower you.

Sometimes, when people have a traumatic experience in their lives, they lose some of their power. The trauma of the experience depletes their energy and they seek to fill the gap with another energy. All too often the other energy they choose is pain. Some people can hold on to pain, such as the pain of childhood abuse, all of their lives. Holding on to pain weakens the heart and can cause long-term depression. What people often do not understand is that if they can learn to let go of their pain, they will experience a sense of joy in their lives that will be beyond anything they have ever known.

If you have been beaten, raped, abused or in any way hurt by another person, mentally or physically holding on to the pain of that experience means that you are choosing to allow that person to have an ongoing negative effect on you. Sometimes this can continue long after the person is dead. If, however, you can learn how to release that deep pain, you will then understand how to let go of all pain. This will give you back the power to be happy, and depression will be a thing of the past.

If you hold on to pain, you hold your Water/heart energies down when they should be up and buoyant. This cuts off your connection to the spiritual world and to all the magic wisdom it contains.

People with weak heart energies are often unable to hear the truth even when it is spoken to them. They stop nourishing themselves and can often suffer from serious insomnia. This is because their minds are full of bad memories — but remember: there is no good or bad until we interact with an energy. If you view something as bad, it is purely how you are viewing it that makes it bad. If you can change your perspective, it can become a good thing. To understand this further, we can use the example that follows.

We all know that children will at some point in their lives experience being burnt. Even if you say to a child, 'Don't touch that, it's hot,' you know that sooner or later curiosity will get the better of the child. A burn can be a very traumatic experience. The pain from a small burn on a finger affects not only the finger, but the whole body. If you look at the burn in isolation, you might say, 'What a terrible thing to happen to that child, if only it could have been avoided.' If, however, you look at the situation objectively, you will see that a relatively small and minor burn can teach a child a respect for fire that may save its life thousands of times. Without that burn, the child would not have learnt an invaluable lesson. When viewed in this manner, the burn is a necessary and ultimately good thing.

It is the same with everything in life. Everything comes to teach you if you know how to learn. Even a deep trauma can empower and teach you and therefore be a good thing. Imagine, if you can learn how to be free of emotional pain for ever, how wonderful life would be. When I work with patients who are holding on to their past pain, to help them get release from it, I tell them to write a letter to whoever caused the pain in them. They don't post the letter; it merely acts as a signal to the sub-conscious mind that the patient wants to release their pain. I then get them to burn the letter whilst imagining giving their pain to the universe. Next I get them to write a letter of forgiveness. This is sometimes hard for the patient to do, but I always say to them that they need to have some compassion for the person. This is because anyone who perpetrates an act of violence or abuse upon another person is sick; they deserve our compassion for they are much further away from their peace and happiness than you or I and will pay the karmic price for their actions — *what you sow is what you reap.* You should also be thankful that you are not them. Meditating on and drawing in the love of the universe that is all around you teaches you how to truly love and respect yourself.

There are positive sides to all of the emotions linked to the four elements once we find balance. The positive side to fear is a different type of fear. If you are gripped by fear, this is negative. If, however, fear is a momentary feeling that kicks your adrenals into working and fires up your inner power, then it is a positive

thing. The positive side to anxiety and judging others is discernment — the ability to discern the truth within others and ourselves;
the positive side to anger is self-motivation; and the positive side
to depression is joy.

Once we learn how to hold the four elements in balance
within ourselves, we will experience all these positive emotions
on a daily and even hourly basis. You can, if you choose to seek
it, have a satisfying life free of fear, depression, anxiety and anger.

The following table summarises the elements and the human
body.

	Earth	**Air**	**Fire**	**Water**	**Ether**
Level	Physical	Mental	Destiny	Emotional	Spiritual
Major organ	Kidneys	Lungs	Liver	Heart	Spleen and pancreas
Other organs	Bladder, adrenals	Large intestine	Gall bladder	Small intestine	Stomach
Tissue	Bones	Skin	Muscles and tendons	Blood and flesh	Blood production and vessels
Orifice	Lower	Nose	Eyes	Ears	Mouth
Emotions	Fear	Anxiety/ judgement	Anger	Depression	Worry

The elements and dependency

One of the games we most commonly play in life is the dependency game. There are four main types of dependency and each
relates to one of the four elements. First is the dependent person
who has Water imbalance. They rely upon other things or people
for their happiness and often form relationships with people who
show a different kind of dependency: co-dependency. A co-
dependent person is someone who feeds another person's dependency, for example, the person who buys an alcoholic a bottle of
whiskey. This type of behaviour is caused by Air imbalance and

is social interaction without learning. People with Earth imbalance are independent or dominant. They like to exert power over others but in doing so they are in danger of alienating themselves, which in turn makes it hard for them to make progress on their spiritual paths. People with Fire imbalance are non-dependent; they cut themselves off from the dependency game, but in doing so risk cutting themselves off from society and the opportunity to learn.

Dependency, like anything else in the universe, is neither good nor bad until we interact with its energy. Each type of dependency has its lesson to teach if we choose to learn it. Independence is bad if it means we become insensitive and unfeeling, but good if it teaches us to stand on our own two feet and hold on to our own power. Dependency is bad if it means that we are endlessly needy, but good if it teaches us the ability to ask for help from others when we need it. Co-dependency is bad if it compounds the problems of others, but good if it teaches us an awareness of the needs of others. Non-dependence is bad if it makes us isolated from opportunities for learning, but good if it teaches us how not to play dependency games.

In terms of dependency, each element represents a game that we play. Earth imbalance leads to power games. This not only includes exerting power over other people, but also engaging in dangerous behaviour in order to prove one's level of power. For instance, someone with Earth imbalance may have a tendency to experiment with drugs. They seek to have fun with drugs. The only problem is that they can end up losing their power and becoming an addict (dependent). Water imbalance leads to 'look-after-me' games. These people rely upon other people or things to make themselves happy when true happiness can only be found within. Fire imbalance leads to a different game. The 'game' is not playing the game. This is often as a result of the person not getting their own way (remember Fire relates to the self). Air imbalance leads to games where individuals seek to feel valued and needed by others. All these games are counter-productive and the best way to stop them is to first recognise which of these

games you play. If you look at yourself honestly, you will probably find that you play them all to some degree in different areas
of your life.

The point of balance — Ether — with regard to dependency is
called interdependence. Interdependent people have the positive
side of all four elements. They can act independently when
required (Earth), but can also accept help from others when they
need it (Water). They are socially aware of the needs of others
(Air) and refuse to play unhealthy dependency games (Fire).

The elements and stress

We all need a time for work (Earth), a time for rest (Water), a time
for self-expression (Fire) and a time for social interaction/
relationships (Air). Stress can develop in any of these areas.

Earth: too much or too little work can be a chief cause of
stress. A further form of work-related stress is having a job that
you do not like. The answer is sometimes to leave your job but
there is another way to counter this type of stress. If you cannot
or do not wish to change your job and yet it stresses you, change
the way that you view it. A change of perspective can often
remove the stress altogether. The most important thing to do if
your work is causing you stress is to initiate change. Ask yourself
'What will it take to make my work better?' and 'What upsets me
about work?' Change the things you can change and change your
perspective towards the things you cannot change.

Water: home should be a place of rest, relaxation and nourishment. Tiredness is a major cause of illness and imbalance and so
rest, relaxation and sound nutrition are essential for health, happiness and fulfilment. If you cannot relax at home, why not try a walk
in the park or in local woodland if you have any? Communing
with Nature is both relaxing and rejuvenating. A candlelit bath is
another good stress-buster. Stress at home can also result from too
little activity or from the after effects of the false highs that some
stimulating drugs can give you.

Fire: stress in this area comes from a lack of personal expression or freedom. This can be as a result of imprisonment but,

equally, can result from the suppression of emotions, which renders the individual a prisoner of their emotions. We all need opportunities for self-expression if we are to remain balanced and healthy. The suppression of the emotions leads to inner stagnation, which is one of the chief causes of cancer in the western world.

Air: stress in this area relates to our social interaction with others, especially in our personal relationships. Most stress in relationships results from misunderstandings and miscommunications. To understand how to remove stress from a relationship, it is worth looking at relationships in terms of the elements.

For a balanced, long-term relationship, you need four things:

- physical or sexual attraction (Earth)
- love and affection (Water)
- shared destiny/goals (Fire)
- shared resources (Air).

To assess a relationship, you can ask the following questions:

- Are you attracted to him/her?
- Is he/she attracted to you?
- Do you like/love him/her?
- Does he/she like/love you?
- Do you share his/her goals?
- Does he/she share your goals?
- Are your lives heading in the same direction?
- Do you have shared values/assets?

If you can answer 'yes' to all these questions, you have a potentially very stable long-term relationship. If there are some 'no's, then it is these areas that need working on. These questions can be adapted to cater for all types of relationships, whether personal or professional.

Often, when I meet couples having relationship problems, I show them the following diagram:

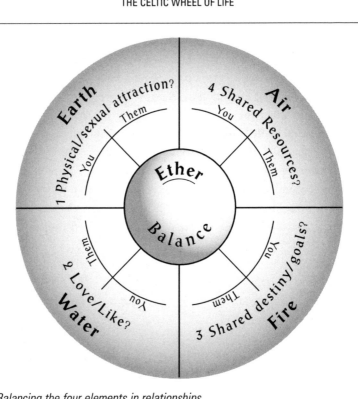

Balancing the four elements in relationships

I draw it out separately for both of them and get them to tick the areas they answered 'yes' to in the questions above. It allows both parties to look more objectively at their relationship and at the needs of the other person. By pinpointing the areas of weakness in terms of the four elements one can quickly see how to resolve them.

Finding balance and harmony

Finding balance and harmony is basically about understanding the interplay between the four elements in all aspects of your life. As I have described the different aspects of the four elements, I am sure that it will have highlighted your own strengths and weaknesses. Weaknesses only manifest in our lives in order to be turned into strengths. In modern society we are taught to suppress our weaknesses but this only depletes our energy and compounds the

problem. The only way to rid yourself of weakness is to first
recognise it within yourself and then seek out ways to turn it into
a strength. The first step in doing this is to understand the nature
of the four elements and how to balance them in your life.

Cycles of growth and learning

The symbol for the four elements is very simple and universally
recognised:

The Celtic symbol for the four elements

It encapsulates the idea of four energies with a central point of
union and is the foundation of Celtic belief and spirituality. The
circle also conveys the idea of movement. We can see this in the
cycles of growth and learning that occur within and around us.
Seasonally the wheel turns from winter (Earth) to spring (Air) to
summer (Fire) and autumn (Water) in a clockwise motion, but

there are other patterns that emerge. In the process of human growth the circle moves the opposite way.

Our lives run in seven-year cycles: the birth of a child is a downward movement and for the first seven years of its life, a child learns how to use its physical body (Earth); from the age of seven to fourteen it learns about emotions and forms a majority of its nutritional preferences (Water); from fourteen to twenty-one it decides what it wants to do in life (Fire); and from twenty-one to twenty-eight it reaches adulthood and learns its place in society (Air). This brings us full circle and the cycle begins again.

It is interesting to note here that it takes approximately twenty-eight years for the planet Saturn to travel around the sun once, which means that every twenty-eight years it is in the same position it was when you were born. This is called the 'Saturn return' and often marks a nodal point in people's lives, as does the age of fifty-six (2 × twenty-eight years).

The problem with modern society is that it tends to frown on personal expression and it attempts to make all individuals conform. This often stops us connecting with our destiny and we never complete the circle and so never gain access to the spiritual wisdom that adulthood should bring. We become stuck and frustrated or, worse still, lose our belief in the power of destiny and abandon our dreams. It is not until we once again learn to flow with the turning of the wheel as our ancestors did that we will find our true place within creation and, with it, our happiness, health and fulfilment.

Wherever you are on your Wheel of Life, it is the energy of Ether that you are looking for. Ether is the middle road, the place of harmony and balance where you are at one with the unfolding universe. It can only be reached through learning humility and acceptance of everything life brings. It is the place of non-judgement where everything just is — rather than being labelled as good or bad. The more you understand about yourself and your interaction with creation around you, the closer you will be to the place of Ether where one is happy, healthy and fulfilled.

Three

THE WHEEL OF THE YEAR

To live a life of harmony, one must be living in harmony with the land. True balance is not just something we seek within ourselves, it means being in tune with all the subtle vibrations of the universe. In the modern world it is sometimes hard to make such connections. Many people remain for ever dissatisfied with life and are disconnected from their true destinies because they do not understand this simple truth. The Celts realised that their very existence was dependent upon the land they lived on that supported them with food and other resources. If crops failed, people starved, and so it was vital that everything possible was done to ensure a good harvest.

One of the chief ways the Celts honoured the land was through the performance of ceremonies at nodal points in the turning cycles of the seasons. The Celts understood that if they were not themselves aligned to the changing energies of the turning year, they were powerless to have a positive effect upon their crops. They also understood that one could not tread a path of true honour and destiny if one was not living in total harmony with the land on which one lived.

Science now tells us that our own bodies change with the turning year. We are sensitive to the amount of sunlight our bodies are exposed to. As the seasons change, hormone levels within our bodies adjust — yet we try to keep everything the same. We attempt to produce the same amount and range of food and work regardless of the time of year. This has the effect of making our own vibration out of harmony with the vibration of the land we live on. This in turn stops us treading our true spiritual path.

A few years ago, I was running a workshop in some ancient woodland near Bath, England. The place is steeped in history and within the woodland are an old Roman bath, an ancient stone circle and an old cave that was reputed once to have been the home of a wise Druid. I took the participants of the workshop on a tour of the woods, including the Druid's cave. When we left the cave Debbie, my partner, said that she had a strong feeling that I and a Celtic wise-woman who had joined us called Eliana should go back into the cave alone. She said that she felt there was something for us to learn from doing so. Eliana and I both checked with our own intuitions and it felt right so the two of us went back into the cave and walked the quarter of a mile to its end. As we were walking down this dark passageway together, I was struck by a sense of history. How many people over the past thousands of years had trod these same steps? I had a sense of many men and women throughout history coming to this special place and feeling the energy of the earth around them in the same manner as I was now. There is something unique about actually being within the earth that always fills me with a sense of wonder.

When we reached the end of the cave we both made ourselves comfortable and quietly sat listening. The air was clear and still and as I sat there with my eyes closed, images began to form in my mind. I saw great gatherings around mighty fires and had a strong sense that I was tapping into ancient vibrations. I felt that the gatherings were very important and that they were about honouring the land. The strongest impression that came into my mind was a message that we, the people who now inhabit the land, should honour the turning of the seasons as our ancestors had. This to me clearly meant celebrating the old festivals that make up the Celtic wheel of the year. After a while the images faded and I was once again aware only of the coolness of the cave. I opened my eyes and asked Eliana her impressions. She talked of similar images to the ones I had seen and said that she too felt we were being told to honour the ancient festivals.

Prior to this time, Debbie and I had lit a fire at some of the Celtic fire festivals and at others had held a celebratory sweatlodge. After this experience I marked all the Celtic fire festivals in my diary and wrote to various friends inviting them to come and celebrate the turning of the year with an evening sweatlodge on the eve of each fire festival. We received a very positive response and so on the eve of the next festival Debbie and I spent the day in preparation. That the first gathering was a magical experience with about twelve of us joining together to do ceremony and to honour each other and our connection to the land. Since then, every festival has been an equally magical and unique experience. Those that have gathered with us have, like us, learnt many lessons whilst having tremendous fun. Sometimes there have been twenty of us, sometimes just Debbie and me, but we have always been deeply rewarded for our efforts. And the more we have done this, the stronger our connection to the land has become. We have learnt a deeper understanding of creation and with it a deeper understanding of ourselves.

Now, eight times a year, on specific days, Debbie and I take time out to honour the turning of the year as our ancestors did. It does not matter what day of the week it is, that day is always put aside as a special day. We are regularly joined by friends and the whole day is set aside as a time for ceremony and honour culminating in an evening gathering to celebrate the turning of the wheel of the year. To us it is an essential part of our lives. It allows us to reconnect our energies to those of the land and this in turn aligns our energies to those of the universe at large because everything in Nature vibrates with the universal energies of creation.

Each festival day in the Celtic calendar honours different aspects of the land and the turning seasons. There are four primary fire festivals:

Samhain	1 November
Imbolc	1 February
Beltane	1 May
Lughnasadh	1 August

Each of these is punctuated either by a solstice or an equinox:

Yule	Winter Solstice, around 21 December
Ostara	Spring or Vernal Equinox, around 20 March
Coamhain	Summer Solstice, around 21 June
Herfest	Autumn Equinox, around 23 September

The Celts recognised that all life begins in darkness (the child in the womb, the seed in the pod) and so every ceremony actually began at dusk on the evening before the festival day. The eve of each festival was a time of both physical and spiritual preparation. Every individual involved in the evening ceremony would spend the day making sure that his or her energy was as balanced and harmonious as possible. They understood that this would allow them to gain the greatest wisdom and empowerment from these special times of celebration and honouring.

I often fast during the day prior to a fire festival as I find it helps to clear and focus my mind. I also make sure that I reconnect with Nature by going for a walk in the woods or by visiting a sacred site. In the lead up to the evening celebration, I can feel different energies around me that give me instruction and insight into how the evening should unfold. We have a Celtic sweatlodge (see Chapter Nine) in the evening where we call upon different energies to help us on our journeys of learning and to prepare us for the path ahead.

To understand the positive effects that reconnecting with the land can have on your life, you have to experience it for yourself. I highly recommend that you take time out, at least in the evening on the eve of each festival, to perform a simple ceremony to honour the turning of the year. Putting your creative energies into a ceremony will reap rich rewards. You may even wish to use a seasonal craft to further help you connect with the energies of creation and I have included some ideas later in the chapter from which you can further develop your own. (You will recognise examples of the four element symbol in these and many other Celtic crafts.)

The following explanations of the meaning and symbolism of each festival comes from my own understanding as I have worked with this path and which has grown deeper each time I have honoured and aligned my energies to the changing season.

Samhain

Samhain (pronounced *SOW-in*) marks the dusk of the year. Just as festival days begin at dusk on the eve of the day, so the Celtic year begins at the dusk of the year. It is the time when the power of darkness is rising in its relentless march towards its time of ultimate power, Yule. Darkness was not regarded by the Celts as something to fear, but as a time when great magic and wisdom could be drawn upon. 31 October, now better known as Halloween, marks the beginning of a three-day festival that runs up until dusk on 2 November. These three days were regarded as a time of 'no-time'. This is because the veil between this reality and other, more subtle realities is very thin and can be easily crossed by those who know how. These other realities are places where the normal laws of time and motion do not exist. It is the land of dreams, the realm of fairies and the little people, of gods and goddesses and of high magic. Celtic shamans would use this time to access the dark realms of this mysterious land, seeking out and forming contacts with the dark energies to empower them through the dark time of the year.

There has been much misunderstanding about the 'Dark Side' since the advent of Christianity. People equate Halloween with demons and evil spirits and thus with Satan and all that is fearful in man. This comes from ignorance and a lack of understanding about the true nature of the universe. There are dark energies in the subtle realms of existence, but they are neither good nor bad until mankind interacts with them. Dark energies tend to be very primal and one needs to be very grounded, balanced and strong-minded to interact with them. This interaction was the job of the Druid or shaman in Celtic times and was certainly not recommended for ordinary folk. Dark energies are very powerful and so have the potential to do great harm if misused or 'played with', but equally they have the potential to do great good if harnessed in the correct manner, with honour and respect.

Samhain was a time of preparation for winter, when excess livestock were killed and salted for the months ahead. Food was always much scarcer during the dark, winter months. It was, at this time, the job of the Druid or shaman to communicate with the rising dark energies at this time. This was in order to understand how to remain in harmony with the coming winter energies so that the land would continue to nourish and support the tribe. The Celts knew that if you did not honour the rising dark energies at Samhain, you could not hope to be honoured by them through- out a potentially harsh winter. Samhain was also a time when the shamans and Druids carried out divinations to allow the tribal members an understanding of their paths ahead so that they could better prepare for any future difficulties or trials.

Whilst the spiritual leaders of a tribe were engaged in a three- day journey into the other realms, the other members of the tribe would be going through their own preparation for the coming months. In ancient Ireland every year, at Samhain, a new sacred fire was lit from which all other fires were kindled. This fire burned throughout the winter to carry the energy of light and life through the dark time of the year until the festival of Beltane.

Samhain was also a time when the dead were honoured. The Celts clearly understood that physical death is merely a rebirth into the realm of spirit and so this honouring of the dead was a time of celebration and feasting, not a time of quiet mourning. At this time, the spirits of the ancestors would be called upon to bestow their wisdom and guidance upon the tribe. Winter's dawn, as it was sometimes called, also marked a time of physical and spiritual consolidation for the Celts. Tools were cleaned, repaired and put away safely for the following spring. Any unresolved issues were sorted out in the mind of each individual (sometimes with the help of the elders of the tribe) so that all could enter this dark time of the year uplifted and empowered.

Winter can be a hard time and hard times challenge us to learn hard lessons. The Celts understood that it was only through being in harmony and balance that such times of difficulty could be overcome. In Ireland it was a tradition at this time to craft a symbol of the four elements called a **parshell** and place it above the door of your home to draw in good energies and as a reminder of the need to be balanced. Without being balanced, they knew that the winter would be much harder. It may seem bizarre to believe that making a parshell from two twigs and some corn stalks could help one survive the winter, but it was much more than a simple seasonal craft. As the cross was being constructed, the maker would be placing their intent for balance and harmony into the craft with his or her mind. This is the foundation of magic and spell-weaving. The mind has great powers that can be harnessed by anyone if they learn how to use it properly. As the craft object was being made, the maker would fill it with thoughts of warm and balancing energies drawing from the energy of the fire and the earth. By the time the object was finished and placed above the door it was vibrant with energies that would shine out positivity throughout the winter months.

A parshell

Making a Samhain Parshell

All you need is two sticks no more than twenty-four inches (60 cm) in length and about a quarter to half an inch (about 1 cm) in diameter, and some straw or ribbon. Fasten the two sticks together in a cross using the straw or ribbon and then weave in and out of the sticks in a sunwise (clockwise) manner. Weave from the middle of the cross outwards until you have about three to four inches (7 to 10 cm) of stick exposed at each end. Remember that your state of mind and the thoughts that you fill it with are of great significance when making any craft object. As you work on your parshell, visualise filling it with positive, beautiful thoughts. Think of summer days in the fields, of the beauty of creation and anything else that fills your heart with joy and light.

━ Weather lore ━

To know if winter shall be cold or warm, go at Samhain to a beech tree, and cut a chip thereof; if it is dry, then the winter shall be warm.

Yule

The festival of Yule (*you-wool*), which begins at dusk on the night before the winter solstice, pre-dates Christianity by several thousand years. Most of the practices that we now associate with Christmas have their roots in pre-Christian traditions, which in turn have deep and meaningful significances. The winter solstice marks the time when the powers of darkness and the energies of the element Earth reach their peak. Many of the animals have gone down to sleep, the nights are long and dark and the whole energy of the season has an insular, downward movement. What better thing to do at this time than lift the spirits with a celebration full of light and splendour?

The imagery attached to this sacred and special time of year is rich with meaning and there are, at this darkest time of year, many messages of hope for the coming spring. Lights were hung up originally to give power to the sun as it began its new season of growth. The red berries of the holly represented the menstrual blood of Mother Earth and the white berries of the mistletoe represented the divine semen of the creator. Ivy, rich with its own berries, also symbolised fertility and the evergreens brought into the house were symbolic of life at this time of darkness and death. In the ancient perpetual battle between the oak king and the holly king, Yule marks the death of the holly king and the birth of the oak king, who will himself 'die' at the summer solstice.

The exchange of gifts often took place at Celtic ceremonies. To the Celts, exchanging gifts was a way of cementing connections with others. They understood that we own nothing. Everything we have is merely borrowed from creation and it will one day return whence it came. Everything that comes into your life is a gift and when it is time for something to leave us, we should let it go with joy, thanking it for its teaching. Gifts, in Celtic times, would have invariably been hand-made by the giver. It might be a medicine tool (such as an animal totem or healing aid), a piece of woven cloth or clothing, or food that had been tended and harvested by the giver. Gifts were like giving someone a piece of your beauty and it was considered a high honour to both give and receive a gift. At Yule there was also the tradition of the gift-bringer. Long before Santa Claus, there was an ancient tradition of the King of Winter (an old, white-haired, bearded gentleman) bringing children a gift in the middle of the night at this time of year. He was always unseen and unheard and it was customary to leave him some food and a glass of wine or ale.

Gifts given at this time were also seen as symbolic of the gifts of wisdom that are to be reaped in the weeks after Yule. This is because the winter solstice is symbolic, not only of death, but also of rebirth. The Celts clearly understood that death to one reality meant birth into a new one, and so it was with the perpetual battle between light and dark. The winter solstice was a time of hope and of looking forward to the lessons that would manifest during the long January nights. These long nights were used to glean wisdom by looking within oneself and back over the past months. The spring would bring new adventures and lessons, so this time was used to make sure that all the wisdom and experience of the past summer and autumn had been properly integrated and understood.

Every festival was accompanied by a feast and none more so than Yule. The best meats and preserves were saved until this time and wine made from the autumn berries was drunk to honour the energies of the past year. Everyone ate their fill, which was especially welcome during harsh winters when food was generally more scarce. The food eaten at the mid-winter feast by the Celts would often be their largest meal until the spring. Having said that, the idea of eating and drinking to excess would have seemed very dishonourable to the Celts. At the end of the festival, everyone felt brighter and more alive, not overfull and exhausted. The feast was designed to empower people and help ward off illness, not to create it through over-indulgence as so often happens in modern society.

Yuletide crafts

There are so many wonderful craft objects that can be made to celebrate this time. The holly wreath and the Christmas tree both have their origins in pre-Christian paganism. They provided a way of bringing the energies of creation into the home at a time when most of Nature is dormant. There are some people who do nothing over the traditional Christmas period out of 'protest' at an ancient pagan festival being highjacked by the Church. I think this is sad. Debbie and I recognise this time of year as a time for joy and celebration. It is not our place to judge others or their beliefs and if we have friends who are celebrating Christmas at the same time that we are celebrating Yule then we celebrate together. We also have a special meal on 25 December. This is not because the day is especially significant to us, but we recognise that it is to many of the people in the western world, so as a mark of respect, we join their celebration. We also join together with friends on 31 December as for us it marks the culmination of ten days honouring and celebration and it is invariably for a simple, quiet meal, not a drunken party.

╔═══╗

━ Weather lore ━

The thirteen days after Yule foretell the weather for the next thirteen lunar months. This means that the weather, both day and night, needs to be taken into consideration. The first day begins at dusk on Yule.

╚═══╝

Imbolc

By Imbolc (IM-bulk), the energies created during the Yule festival had often waned over the sometimes harsh and dreary January weeks. Imbolc brought new hope and cheer during a month that could also seem long and dull. During February the power of the sun is growing day by day but it has not gained enough strength to banish the cold of winter. Imbolc welcomes the dawn of spring as signified by the birth of the first lambs and the blooming of the woodland snowdrops.

Imbolc is a festival sacred to the goddess Brighid, the 'exalted one'. She is a 'triple' goddess, with three aspects — maiden, mother and crone — representing the three aspects of woman-hood — healing, fertility and knowledge. In her many and varied forms, she was linked to the powers of the moon. This festival was an empowerment ritual that honoured women. To the Celts, women were regarded as equal to men. They were not, however, regard-ed as the same as men. Women were, and still are, the keepers of the most ancient wisdom. They, through their monthly menstrual cycle, embody creation. When a woman menstruates, her energy becomes very grounded by the downward flow of her blood. This allows her access to higher realms of wisdom. A woman in her 'moon-time' was regarded by the Celts as highly honoured and her wisdom was always listened to with openness and humility. Imbolc honoured this attitude to women.

The festival began at dusk on 31 January although the sacred fire was often not lit until dawn the following morning. It was the first of a trio of festivals that marked the increasing power of the sun and creation, the other two being Ostara and Beltane. Imbolc comes at a time when the first glimpses of new life can barely be seen. It marks a time when the introspection of winter should cease and the mind should be put to work formulating plans for the coming spring season. In Celtic times much of this planning would have revolved around farming, but it also applies to our own spiritual 'pastures' where we grow new insights and under-standings.

Because Brighid is a goddess of the moon, Imbolc was also linked to water. It was a time when sacred, healing wells were honoured with gifts, candles and offerings. The healing powers of spring water were well known to the Celts and were used as the basis of many of their herbal medicines. Honouring the sacred wells was a way of returning energy to the well so that it would continue to imbue its waters with healing vibrations. Sacred wells were nearly all sacred to local goddesses and were honoured with a small offering whenever they were drawn from, but Imbolc marked a time when everyone could gather together and give thanks with one accord.

➤ Weather lore ➤

If Imbolc is dry and fair, half of winter's yet to come and more; if Imbolc is wet and foul, half the winter's gone at Yule.

Brighid's eye

At this time of year, a craft object called 'Brighid's eye' was made. It is crafted the same as a parshell, except brightly coloured threads or wool are used. Take a straight piece of hazel, no more than two feet (60 cm) long and half an inch (1 to 2 cm) thick, and cut it in half. Take the two pieces and tie them together in the middle with a piece of wool. Weave the wool in and out of the crosspieces in either a clockwise or anti-clockwise direction. Once a good sec-tion of colour has been created, tie on a different coloured piece of wool and weave a section with that before changing colour again. You can use up to eight different colours and the end result can be stunning. Once made it can be used to decorate an altar, any part of the house or left as an offering at a sacred well.

Ostara

Ostara (*oss-tara*), the spring equinox, is the second of the three spring festivals. It marks a nodal point in the turning of the year when the power of the light first gains true ascendance over the power of darkness. Cernunnos, lord of the animals, and the Green Man, master of the forest, were both honoured at this time. The new buds were breaking open and the mating season was just beginning. The energies created at Imbolc were now consolidated to ensure fertility to the land and the animals.

Ostara marks the time when the energies of light and dark, male and female are equal. This festival symbolised the sacred mating between the Celtic god and goddess so that she may conceive a sun-child to be born nine months later at the winter solstice. It marked the beginning of the planting season, both physically and spiritually. It was thus a time of high activity when a great deal of energy and attention was heaped upon the new seedlings to ensure that they matured to bear fruit.

Ostara is essentially a fertility rite symbolising the production of the egg. At Imbolc, the energies to produce the egg are stirred. At Ostara the egg is formed and at Beltane the egg is fertilised. The painting of eggs is another pre-Christian tradition that has direct links to this cycle of spring festivals. Both the hare and the rabbit, well known for their high fertility, have long been honoured at this time. Modern versions revolve around the Easter Bunny and Easter Egg but much of the true symbolism is lost to modern people and with it is lost their chance to renew their connection to the land.

This idea of the developing egg transfers to many levels beyond the physical. Spiritually Ostara marks a time of transition away from the introspection before Imbolc and towards the new enlightenments that come with Beltane. This was indeed a powerful time that today is often lost amidst chocolate and passion plays.

Hot cross buns

There was a pre-Christian tradition on the morning of Ostara for women to rise early and make a spiced cake of wheaten flour, marked with a cross upon it. It was made to a special recipe and was said to have special curative powers, especially for stomach illness (dysentery, diarrhoea and summer sickness) and whooping cough. It was also said never to go mouldy. Several buns were always set aside and hardened in the oven and hung up until they were needed. When any illness came, the bun would be finely grated and mixed with goat's milk or water as a medicine. The Saxons too ate a similar traditional cake at this time. The Christian tradition of eating hot cross buns on Good Friday dates only as far back as 1361. They were given to the poor at St. Albans Abbey at Ostara that year and it is said that the tradition originated then and grew. The monks at that time almost certainly knew of the curative powers of the buns and probably based theirs on a version of the ancient recipe.

Egg painting
The tradition of egg painting goes back at least as far as the Celts and probably beyond. Throughout the world, the egg is the universal symbol of fertility. In Celtic times at Ostara, eggs were hard-boiled, dyed bright colours and often elaborately painted. If you would like to try this, boil an egg in water with an onion skin added and it will dye the shell a rich yellow colour. Alternatively, put some petals, a small flat flowerhead or a fern leaf against the shell, tie onion skin around it and parcel it in a white cloth before boiling. The imprint of the leaf or flower is then left upon the golden shell. There are many other plants that can be used to produce beautiful dyes, such as woad and extracts from trees (see Chapter Five).

➤ Weather lore ➤

When the clouds look like rocks and towers, the earth will be refreshed by spring showers.

Beltane
Beltane (*bal-ten-a*) marks the beginning of summer and is heralded by the flowering of the May tree or Hawthorn. Another

name for Beltane is **Cetsamhain** and it stands opposite Samhain in both the wheel of the year and in significance. It is a festival of light symbolising the union between the masculine and feminine energies of the land, the Lord of the Greenwood and the Queen of the May. In Britain this union is still recognised in the traditional May Day celebrations such as crowning the May Queen and dancing round the Maypole.

Just as Samhain represents the dusk of the year, so Beltane represents the dawn. Both times were recognised by the Celts as times when the veil between this world and the other worlds was very thin. Beltane was particularly noted as a time for seeing and communicating with the fairy world. If you venture into ancient woodland at this time of year, you are likely to find circles of fungi growing beneath the spreading canopy. These are known as 'fairy rings' and they are said to mark the place where fairies dance in the nightly celebrations that take place within that realm at this time. The Celts believed that the land of fairy and the land of dreams were one in the same and that this was another realm that existed in the same physical space as we do, but at a higher vibration. It can best be perceived when the mind is in a daydream state similar to when we are on the edge of sleep.

It was shortly after Beltane 1999 that I was writing this section of this book. When I am writing a book, I always take regular walks in Nature to help and inspire me. When I was writing this section, I arose early one morning and decided to go for a leisurely walk in a small piece of ancient woodland near where I live. The woods were full of amazing beauty. The hawthorn was in full bloom, as were the bluebells and wild garlic. The scent was heavenly and very relaxing. It was a warm, damp day, the sort that often comes in early May in south-west England and as I strolled along I felt as though I was being bathed in the energies of creation around me. My intuition told me to take a path that I hadn't taken for over a year and as I walked around a bend in the path I was met by a sea of blooms. Beside the path and stretching into the woodland were bluebells, wild garlic, pink campion, lesser celandine and wild primroses.

It was then that I noticed a fairy ring surrounding part of a badger set. I walked around the ring for a while trying to decide whether or not to enter it. I mentally asked permission to enter the ring and, as my intuition gave me no negative signs, I stepped inside and crouched down. I felt an urge to close my eyes and as I did so images came to mind of little people, each about the size of a small child and dressed in green and brown clothes. They were riding on the backs of badgers and appeared to be having a very enjoyable time. I could not tell whether the badgers were aware of the fairies or not but the animals too seemed to be enjoying themselves.

The energy of the fairy world is subtle and cannot be perceived with the conscious, left-brain mind. One has to learn to quieten the left brain and open up the intuitive right brain if one wants to have encounters with fairy folk. Are encounters like the one I mention above perceptions of another real world or the product of human imagination? I don't think it matters. If you perceive something, whether in this physical world or in any other world, that has a real effect upon you, it must be real at some level.

The lighting of Beltane fires on hilltops and in sacred places was an important ritual throughout the Celtic lands. These fires, called 'needfires', were used to drive cattle through, or between two separate fires, as a means of securing immunity to disease. The fire would be constructed in a sacred manner and would have offerings made to it, for example, herbs, animal artefacts or totems to imbue the fire with powers that would then be passed on to the cattle. People traditionally leapt over Beltane fires to be filled with the same powerful energies. In Britain, nine men would bring nine different woods to kindle the Beltane fire. Nine was a number of great potency to the Celts and is mentioned often in Celtic mythology. Originally the fires were lit around a single sacred tree or upright pole which had been decorated with greenery and flowers to represent the union of the energies of the Lord of the Greenwood and the Queen of May. This was the precursor to the Maypole.

Beltane marks the death of winter and this was celebrated with feasting and dancing. In her book, *British Folk Customs*, Christina

Hole writes about an ancient custom in the Isle of Man which continued well into the eighteenth century. The Queen of May, a local young lady, engaged in a mock battle with the Queen of Winter, played by a man dressed in women's clothing. Each side had 'troops' dressed in attire representing summer and winter and they did battle on a local common. If the Queen of May was kidnapped, a ransom equivalent to the cost of the day's festivities had to be paid. The day was then rounded off with feasting and dancing.

Another Beltane practice was gathering dew on May Day morning. A traditional English rhyme goes:

A fair maid who, the first of May
Goes to the fields at break of day
And washes in dew from a hawthorn tree
Will ever after handsome be.

The practice was not limited to hawthorn trees but to any dew gathered on May Day morning. On 1 May 1515, Queen Catherine of Aragon is recorded to have gone to the fields with twenty-five of her ladies in waiting and Samuel Pepys, the famous English diarist, records his wife and her maid doing the same thing in 1669. The dew was also said to have special healing properties and was used to treat consumption, goitre, physical weakness and a whole host of other ills.

Making a May crown

This traditional craft was created, not only to adorn the May Queen, but also as an offering to Beltane fires and as a decoration for May Day feasting tables. Traditionally it was constructed by weaving a small piece of flowering hawthorn in a circle and attaching flowers to it with coloured cloth. If you do not have access to hawthorn, you can use a wire ring and tie flowers on to it with coloured ribbons. I need give no more detailed instructions as to how the crown should be made as it is meant to be a unique creation inspired by the energies of Nature. It does not matter so much how the crown turns out, more the intent and thoughts that you put into it as you make it and it is these that will dictate its beauty.

➤ Weather lore ➤

Observing the budding of the oak and ash tree at Beltane gives a good indication of rainfall in the summer to come, as this old rhyme tells: 'Oak before ash, we're in for a splash; ash before oak and we're in for a soak.'

Coamhain

Coamhain, the summer solstice, marks the longest day of the year and has been a traditional day for grand tribal gatherings since ancient times. Many of the pre-Celtic stone circles and other monuments are aligned to the rising sun on the morning of Coamhain, including Stonehenge. It marks the time when the sun is at its most powerful and creation is at its most active. It is also the time when the oak tree flowers; the energy of the oak tree was especially honoured at this time.

Many plants and trees are at their peak of growth in the month of June. This was the time between planting and harvesting when the fields and woods were abundant with flowers, but, for the Celts, it was not a time of rest. Herbs were gathered and dried to be stored for use throughout the year and midsummer's eve was a traditional time for wand-cutting. The most sacred herb to the Druids, mistletoe was also gathered at this time in a special ceremony. Mistletoe was regarded as a very special plant because it grew 'between heaven and earth' as a parasite on trees and it had a reputation as a 'heal-all'. It grows on several different types of tree, but the most sacred was that growing on the king of trees, the oak. Mistletoe was also regarded as a protection against lightning and this may be due to the fact that it is attracted to the oak just as lightening is. The oak is one of the forest trees most likely to be struck by lightning. It is probable that the Celts knew that like repels like and so surmised that if mistletoe and lightening were both attracted to the same tree, they would not be attracted to one another.

➳ Weather lore ➳

If dandelions do not open on the morning, expect rain.

Wand-cutting

Trees have been used as a source of magical tools since before the discovery of metals, and midsummer's eve, when the sap is at its height, is a special time for cutting wands. Wands were used by the Celts in many different ways including for marking out ceremonial circles and as energy directors in healing ceremonies. Hazel is often favoured for wands due to its straight branches although you may choose wood from any tree that you feel drawn to. Mentally ask the tree's permission to use some of its wood by first making physical contact with the tree and then thinking or asking out loud for permission to take some of its wood. You should explain to the tree that you need its wood for a magical tool and ask it to leave a part of its energy in the piece you are to cut. If the answer that comes to mind is positive cut a length of wood. If the answer is negative, find another tree. The more you work with trees in this way, the clearer the responses will be. It is difficult to explain how these responses come to mind but the easiest way to judge whether you are getting a positive or negative response is by how you feel inside. If you feel a sense of peace and harmony, then the answer is positive. If, however, you feel any sense of something not being quite right, you should always err on the side of caution and either seek another tree or seek further confirmation.

Some traditions say that a wand should measure the same as the distance from your elbow to the tip of your forefinger and no more than half an inch (1 to 2 cm) in diameter although I cut different sized wands for different purposes according to my intuition. After you have cut the branch, leave a small token of thanks such as tying a ribbon to the tree or leaving a crystal by its base. Once you get the wand home, if you don't want the bark on it you should strip it off whilst the wood is fresh and then leave it to dry before decorating it in whatever way you feel is appropriate. It is always best to follow your intuition when deciding how to decorate a wand. You may wish to burn or paint designs upon it, tie ribbons on it or just leave it in its natural state.

Lughnasadh

This festival (pronounced *Loo-nass-ah*), beginning on the eve of 1 August, was a warrior's cere-mony to prepare the hunters of the tribe for the coming months when they would venture out and hunt game to be salted for the winter. Its associations with the warrior energy are probably due to the fact that it is said that the Fir Bolg, a Celtic warrior tribe, first arrived in Ireland on 1 August. Lughnasadh, or 'Lammas' as it is sometimes called, was a very primal affair with participants donning animal masks and skins to help them attune better to the energies of the animal world and performing tests of strength and endurance for personal empowerment. At the end of the festival, men and women would sometimes paint a spiral on their chests using woad. Woad produces a strong blue dye and the spiral would remain on the skin until the next festival reminding them of the spiral of creation that comes to full fruition at Herfest.

Lughnasadh also marked the beginning of harvesting, especially corn. It is sacred to the sun god, Lugh, and is known in Ireland as the 'first fruits' festival. Lughnasadh literally means 'the games of Lugh'. Legend tells us that Lugh's foster-mother, Tailtui, was a member of the Fir Bolg and it is said that after her death, one 1 August, Lugh declared that the day should be set aside as a sacred day to honour the memory and wisdom of his mother. Traditionally it became an annual sports festival but there were many other practices associated with this time. In Ireland and Scotland, any handfastings (marriages) performed on 1 August were said to last a year and a day. After a year the couples would either renew their vows for another year or go their separate ways. It was also a time of general merriment and love-making designed to create positive energies to encourage a rich and bountiful harvest.

Lughnasadh was a time to honour the spirit of the corn and other grains. It traditionally marked the symbolic death of the spirit of the corn and fields were harvested in such a way as to corner the corn spirit into the last remaining piece of uncut corn. This piece was cut ceremonially, woven into a corn dolly (see below) and decorated with coloured ribbon to honour Demeter, the Corn Mother. The dolly would then be affixed to the barn to ward off lightning or given place of honour on the mantelpiece or hearth, which was used as an altar in ancient times.

In many parts of the Celtic lands, it was considered unlucky to be the one to cut the last remaining stalk of corn because it caused the death of the corn spirit. To avoid bad luck, all the reapers would gather round the last stalk and simultaneously throw their sickles at the base of the corn so that no one would know who was responsible for slaying the corn spirit.

⬤ Weather lore ⬤
When trees show the underside of their leaves (making them lighter in appearance) or if an owl hoots more than once during the day, it is a sign of coming wet weather.

How to make a traditional corn dolly
This is the most complicated of all the craft items included in this section and takes time and patience to master. You will need a pair of scissors or a knife, a pen, five long pieces of straw with heads, several straws without heads, some straw-coloured thread and coloured ribbon.

1. Cut the five pieces of straw with heads just above where the leaf nearest to the head joins the stalk. Using the thread, tie all five pieces together just below the heads and spread the stalks out evenly. With the pen number the straws from 1 to 5 in an anti-clockwise direction (see Figure 1).

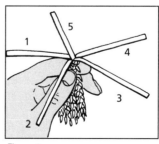
Figure 1

2. Holding the heads carefully in one hand, take straw 1 in the other hand and bend it over 2 and 3 so that it lies between 3 and 4. Now turn the whole thing a quarter-turn clockwise.

3. Bend 3 over 1 and 4 so that it lies between 4 and 5 (see Figure 2). Bend 4 over 3 and 5. Bend 5 over 4 and 2.

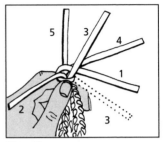

Figure 2

4. Bend 2 over 5 so that it lies parallel to 1 (see Figure 3).

5. Bend 1 under and round 2 so that it lies parallel with 3 (see Figure 4).

6. Bend 3 under and round 1 so that it lies parallel to 4. Continue this process with successive straws.

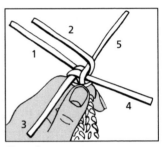

Figure 3

7. As the weave widens out keep adjusting the position of your hands so that the weave is held securely in place (see Figure 5).

8. When you have nearly reached the end of a piece of straw, attach a new piece by pushing the thin end of the new piece into the hollow end of the old piece and then continue weaving.

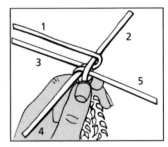

Figure 4

9. When the dolly is half the length you want, start to decrease the width by overlapping the straws as you weave them (see Figure 6).

10. As you near the end, make sure you have three straws that will be at least eight inches (20 cm) long once you have finished your weave. Cut and add new pieces of straw as necessary to achieve this.

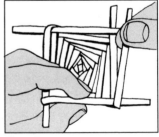

Figure 5

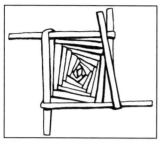

Figure 6

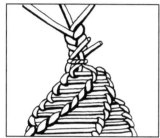

Figure 7

11. When the weave is complete, tie the remaining straws tightly at the top of the weave with thread and begin to plait the three long straws. These will form the loop at the top (see Figure 7).

12. Bend the finished plait into a loop and secure it to the two remaining shorter pieces of straw using the thread. Trim the end and decorate the bottom with ribbon (see Figure 8).

Figure 8

Herfest

The final festival of the Celtic year is held at the autumn equinox and is called Herfest (*her-vest*). It marks the culmination of the year's efforts when the fruits of one's labours are gathered in. It was traditionally a time of great feasting to celebrate the gifts provided by Mother Nature and to honour the energies of the land and sky that had nourished the plants so that they could produce a bountiful harvest.

The harvest supper was held at the end of the harvesting after what was perhaps the time of greatest work for the Celts. It was vital that all the fruits and grains were safely gathered in and stored before the autumn winds and rains came. Everyone would work long hours and so the feast was a reward for everyone's hard work. After the feast, which would include game, poultry, fish, breads, vegetables, fruits, cider and ale, there would be singing and dancing until dawn.

The time from Herfest until Samhain was a time of 'bedding down' the animals and the land for the winter ahead. Everyone's minds would have been on the coming New Year, a time of endings and new beginnings, of death and rebirth. As the nights drew in, so the thoughts of the people would turn inwards, reflecting on the lessons and adventures of the past months and preparing for the cold season with its new teachings and wisdom. Everyone would be able to look back over a year of learning and achievement, because everyone who learns to live in harmony with the land and the turning seasons cannot fail to gain in wisdom and understanding.

Weather lore

If onion skin is very thin, a mild winter is coming in. If onion skin is thick and tough, the coming winter will be cold and rough.

At this time Nature is so abundant and bountiful that you can use your imagination to create your own unique craft item. You can use feathers, wood, corn, barley, fruits, berries and a whole host of other natural things. The best way to do this is to go out into the countryside and collect whatever calls out to you. Once back home, you can ask the items themselves how they want to be crafted and let thoughts, images and ideas fill your imagination. Remember that it is the intent with which you make something that dictates the beauty of the finished item.

The Celtic Great Year

The Celts honoured the energies of both the sun and the moon as representations of the masculine and feminine. They had a deep knowledge of astronomy and of the cycle of the sun, moon and planets. The eight Celtic festivals run on a solar calendar but it is well known that the Celts observed the lunar calendar as well. The Celtic lunar calendar has thirteen months each of twenty-eight days, making exactly 364 days, but the cycle of the moon is not exactly twenty-eight days. The solar year is not exactly 364 days either, so there is an anomaly in both cycles. The lunar and solar calendars usually run slightly out of phase with each other but approximately every nineteen years they are in a position of co-incidence. The Celts knew that the cycles of the sun and moon come into phase approximately every nineteen years and so marked a 'Great Year' which spanned nineteen years starting and ending with a lunar eclipse.

The actual cycle of coincidence runs every 18.61 years, which means that true coincidence between the sun and moon takes place only every fifty-six years, made up from two cycles of nine-teen years and one of eighteen years. At the end of every fifty-six years, the Celts held a major festival that lasted at least a week and coincided with a lunar eclipse.

Gerald Hawkins in his book, *Stonehenge Decoded*, demonstrates a strong argument to prove that this knowledge came from the pre-Celtic builders of Stonehenge. He believes that they marked the Great Year with posts around the central circle and he shows that every fifty-six years a lunar eclipse was visible exactly over the heel stone. Certainly the priests of that time would have been aware of this phenomenon and would have regarded it as highly significant.

The cycles of nineteen and fifty-six years were important to the Celts and were marked by huge gatherings and ceremonies, but of perhaps greater importance was the year-by-year cycle that gave them their connection to the land. Honouring the eight Celtic festivals is an excellent way to reconnect with the energies of creation and makes the perfect starting-point from which to ex-plore Celtic spirituality. You don't have to do anything elaborate or complicated, but there is real value in putting the day aside to do ceremony. You could start as Debbie and I did by lighting a sacred fire on the evening of the eve of each festival and perhaps collect things from the wild and make a craft item. The most important thing is to follow your intuition. There is no right or wrong way of doing things and provided you work from a per-spective of love and respect you can do no harm.

The Celtic sacred fire

When the Celts built a sacred fire it was a whole ceremony in itself. Fire is one of the most powerful and primal of all the energies of the universe. If harnessed and treated with respect it can provide warmth, healing and purification, but if met with ignorance it can burn and destroy with speed and ferocity. Fire embodies the primal energy of life and death as can be seen by the abundance of new green shoots that emerge after a forest fire. It was central to most Celtic ceremonies.

Your state of mind and the manner in which you build a fire has a marked bearing on its power and effectiveness as a tool in ceremony. I cannot tell you how to build a sacred fire because the manner is unique to each individual, but I can share with you some thoughts and ideas from my own experience of building fires for ceremony.

The size and shape of the fire depends on the size of the ceremony and the available space. Every fire is unique and the best guide is your intuition. How you build a fire also depends upon what you are honouring and what energies you want to call in. Every piece of wood has its own energy and vibration that contributes to the overall energy of the fire as does your every thought and intent. If I want to make a small fire, for example, to honour the moon, I often use only thirteen pieces of wood representing the thirteen lunar months of the year. I build them into a square tower using two pieces of wood laid parallel about eight to twelve inches (20 to 30 cm) apart for each storey with a single piece of wood on the top. I then add paper and kindling, followed by prayers and offerings, before lighting it.

At Beltane you may like to build a fire around a centrally decorated pole to represent the Maypole and at Yule on a base of coal to represent the deep and dark energies that rise at that time of year. You may also wish to construct a simple altar by the fire on which to place offerings or special objects that need to be cleansed or empowered with the energies of the fire. The more you build a sacred fire around the symbolism of the ceremony the more powerful it will be. As you learn more on your spiritual path you will naturally transfer that knowledge into your fire-building and it will evolve into your own unique 'medicine'.

The Celts offered sea-salt as it was seen as the sacred embodiment of the four elements, being of the earth, coming from the water, created through the evaporation by the fire of the sun, allowing the sea-water to rise into the air and leaving the salt behind. They would offer the salt to the four cardinal directions, to the sky above, the ground below and to the creator whose spark is in each and every one of us.

The prayers said during these offerings were to call upon the help of the energies of creation and were usually created in the moment rather than rehearsed or read from a book. Again your best guide is your own intuition but to give you some ideas here is a typical pattern that I use to build a sacred fire.

I first clear the ground of any debris and then begin to construct a simple base by placing chopped pieces of wood side by side. The number of pieces is dictated by the symbolism I am using and each piece of wood is mentally thanked for its energy and sacrifice before being put in place. I then build the fire following my intuition and add paper and kindling. When the fire is ready for lighting, I take some sea-salt in my right hand and, holding it up towards the North say:

> Creator, Great Spirit, I offer this sacred salt to the North and call upon the energies of the North wind to help me with this fire. And I call upon the power of Earth to ground me and banish all fear.

I then place the salt on the part of the fire facing North.

I turn to the East taking some more salt and, offering it up in the direction of the East, say:

> Creator, Great Spirit, I offer this sacred salt to the East and call upon the energies of the East wind to help me with this fire. And I call upon the power of Air to allow me to draw in the learning and understanding I need.

I then place the salt on the part of the fire facing East.

Turning to the South I once again hold up salt and say:

> Creator, Great Spirit, I offer this sacred salt to the South and call upon
> the energies of the South wind to help me with this fire. And I call upon
> the power of fire to purify my thoughts and allow me to freely express
> my energy.

Having placed the salt on the South side, I turn to the West and,
salt in hand, say:

> Creator, Great Spirit, I offer this sacred salt to the West and call upon
> the energies of the West wind to help me with this fire. And I call upon
> the power of Water to cleanse and uplift me.

I take some salt and bend to touch and connect with the ground
saying:

> Creator, Great Spirit, I offer this sacred salt to Grandmother Earth and
> call upon the energies of the plants, stones and animals to help
> me with this fire. And I ask for a deeper understanding of these my
> brothers and sisters

and place the salt in the North-West. I take some salt and, holding it heavenwards, say:

> Creator, Great Spirit, I offer this sacred salt to Grandfather Sky and call
> upon the energies of the spirit world to help me with this fire. And I call
> upon my spirit guides to instruct and guide me

and place the salt in the North-East. Finally I take some salt and
holding it over my heart say:

> Creator, Great Spirit, I offer this sacred salt to you and the
> creative spark you have placed within me. Guide and guard me on this
> path and teach me to love everything as you do, without condition.

I then place the salt in the centre of the fire. Finally, I add other offerings such as herbs or tobacco and light the fire using a single match.

This is how I typically create a sacred fire but it is not a set of rules for you to follow, only a guideline. How you build your own fires is up to you. You can light it with one match or a hundred and can use the offering pattern I have shown you or create your own. Some people just make the sign of a circle over the fire and offer one simple prayer whilst others go through an elaborate set of prayers and rituals. It is really up to you. The only important rules are to follow your own intuition and to do everything with love and respect for yourself and creation around you.

Four

FINDING TRUE BALANCE

The Celts were connected to creation at every level. They sought always to be in balance with Nature because they understood that it was the only way to find true harmony. In Nature there is no cancer, multiple sclerosis, irritable bowel syndrome or osteoporosis. In fact in the world of Nature, where man has not intervened or influenced, there is neither disease nor imbalance. What makes us different? I believe that we have forgotten the most fundamental truth that you are what you eat. If you want to live in harmony and balance with creation around you, if you want to perceive the subtle realms of existence, your vibration has to be in harmony with the land. If you are seeking a true understanding of yourself and Nature it can only be found if you live and eat with the land.

If you put an Eskimo, living in the arctic, on a citrus-only diet, he or she would almost certainly die within a few days or weeks. The cause of death would most probably be either hypothermia or a heart attack due to too much fluid around the heart. This is because citrus fruit has natural chemicals within it that cool the body down and make it retain more fluid. In a tropical climate this is essential because the body needs to retain water so that it can sweat to keep cool. If you put someone living in a tropical country on a diet of seal meat and whale blubber, they too would almost certainly die in a short time. This time the cause of death would most probably be either heat exhaustion or a heart attack due to dehydration of the heart. This is because seal meat and whale blubber warm the body and clear it of potentially cooling excess fluid. Again, this is essential in an arctic climate to prevent hypothermia.

Nature provides, in any given climate, a clear indication of what foods should be eaten by people living in that climate. It is impossible in Britain, in the middle of winter, to go out into Nature or into your back garden and pick a banana or an orange off a tree. These fruits are virtually impossible to grow in this country and especially in winter. Even if you could get a banana tree to grow naturally in Britain it would never yield fruit. Such trees grow in hot climates and their fruits contain natural chemicals to cool the body. If you eat these fruits in the middle of winter in a temperate climate, you over-cool the body making it much more susceptible to attack from bacteria and viruses. There is always an outbreak of colds, flu and other illnesses just after the Christmas festivities and this is due to the fact that we are out of balance with creation around us. If you eat in harmony with the land you develop the strength and power to be able to resist the attack of bacteria and viruses.

In the west we seem under the illusion that bacteria and viruses are stronger than we are and that we will all inevitably fall victim to their attack sooner or later. This is not true. All microorganisms need very specific circumstances in order to thrive. Many bacteria and viruses can only exist in the human body when it is overly acidic. We should eat 80 per cent alkaline foods and only 20 per cent acid foods. However, sugar, artificial additives, most processed foods, tea, coffee and alcohol are all acidic and often the average western diet is so acidic as to be a veritable breeding ground for bugs. Furthermore, most bacteria and viruses thrive in an oxygen-deficient environment. If you have a good level of oxygenation in your blood, it is impossible for bacteria and viruses to get a hold. The modern-day problem is that our blood is so full of toxins that it cannot carry enough oxygen to keep us healthy. Toxins appear in the form of pesticide residues, nitrates, artificial colourings, flavour enhancers, preservatives and a whole host of other unnatural substances. On top of that, most westerners have forgotten how to breathe properly and so are also not taking enough oxygen into their bodies.

Fundamentally though, all illness begins in the mind. We become weak because of unhealthy thinking habits, many of which revolve around food. From the moment a child is told, 'Stop crying and I'll give you a sweetie,' it is being taught to rely upon food for its happiness and comfort. If you cannot start the day without a cup of tea or coffee, you are giving your power away to that substance. If you cannot imagine a day without chocolate or tobacco or alcohol, then you are addicted to these substances and will never find your path to happiness and fulfilment until you take back your power. If you are addicted to anything, you are giving your power away to that addiction by relying upon it for support. Your happiness has become dependent upon you having your 'fix'. This is not a healthy way to run a life.

The body is the temple of the soul. Without the body, the soul has no expression. Everything you put into your mouth has an effect upon your body's biochemistry and therefore upon your mind. The body speaks only a natural language, not a synthetic one. If I took a photograph of a tree trunk, blew the picture up to life-size and put it next to the tree, you would easily be able to tell the difference. If I said, 'They look the same, therefore they are the same,' you would probably reply, 'You are mistaken because one is an image and the other is alive.' Modern scientists, doctors and food technologists miss this simple truth. They view chemical chains, whether from a natural source or synthetic, as the same thing. They are not. One is a flat, lifeless facsimile and the other is vibrant with the energies of creation.

Many scientists even now agree that substances, such as monosodium glutamate (a common flavour enhancer), are not good for you and still we poison ourselves with them. We treat our temple like a rubbish tip, filling it with 'stuff' rather than with the harmonising energy of creation. One patient of mine once said to me, 'Everything comes from creation in some way and therefore everything is good for you if you tune into its energy.' I replied, 'If that is true, why not eat your food in the middle of a nuclear reactor?' Just because everything is a part of creation does not mean that it is good for human beings. A speeding truck is, on one level, a part of creation but if you see one heading towards you, you do not open your arms and say 'Welcome into my life, truck, I acknowledge you as a part of creation and seek to learn all I can from you.' Of course not, you get out of the way as quickly as possible. You use a gift called 'common sense', one that we seem to have forgotten to use when it comes to thinking about our nutrition.

There are foods that can empower you and foods that can weaken you. Neither is good or bad until human beings interact with them. Common sense tells you not to eat arsenic because you know it is a poison, and yet so many people fill their bodies full of slow-acting poisons through not using common sense when choosing what to eat. Everyone knows in their own heart that pesticides and synthetic chemicals are not good for us. If we could tune into our intuition, if we could truly listen to our senses, we would know that the foods that are commonly available in the western world are poisoned. We would also know that it is these unnatural substances that take us away from our true connection with creation. If you want to honour the land, you must first honour your body. If you want to make those people around you happy, you must first find true happiness yourself and this can only be achieved when you learn balance.

True happiness is a state of being that can potentially be found in any circumstance. It is not dependent upon anything or anyone. You should be able to have inner peace and happiness whether you are eating a banquet or a plain bowl of oats and water, whether you are wracked with pain or free from all symptoms. This happiness is not euphoria because euphoria is not balance. True happiness is an inner joy and acceptance of everything that manifests into your life. It comes when you understand that everything that manifests into your life is potentially good and empowering for you if you embrace it and learn from it. Again that understanding only comes through learning how to live in harmony with creation around you.

The Celts, like all other indigenous people of the world at that time, ate in harmony with the seasons because they ate from the land. They did not have daily deliveries of fruit and coffee from Africa and South America. Mother Nature never catered for a free market economy. She provides in any given climate, when unmolested by modern agriculture, the perfect balance of grains, fruits and vegetables for the nourishment and health of the people living in that climate. Common sense tells us that if a food grows naturally on the land, in this climate, the probability is that it will be better for you than the same food grown thousands of miles away in a foreign climate. In the same way, food eaten in harmony with the seasons has to be better for you than food eaten out of season. In Britain, in the autumn and through the winter, lots of root vegetables grow — swede, turnip, onion, parsnip and more. These foods all have warming properties, perfect for the cold winter nights. Nature shows us clearly the path of harmony and balance if we choose to follow her guidance and use our common sense.

The Celts would have regarded our modern eating habits as primitive and barbaric. They would be horrified at the lack of respect we show both for creation and our own bodies. They would have seen us as gluttons eating far more food than we really need. There was no obesity amongst the Celts because they rarely ate until they were full. Unlike us, the Celts would have spent a large part of their lives hungry. This does not mean that they were impoverished and starving. There is a difference between being hungry and starving. The habit of eating until you are full, or until you are *too* full, came to the Celtic lands via the Romans. Prior to that time, eating to capacity was reserved only for one or two of the festival feasts. The reason for this is that if you regularly eat to capacity, you regularly have that satisfied and comfortable feeling which leads to sluggishness and stagnation. Our ancestors knew that overeating dulls the senses and, at that time, this could threaten your survival. Nowadays, with convenience stores and modern supermarkets, we actually have to do very little to survive and this has led to stagnation and ill health.

One should only ever eat to 80 per cent capacity — remaining hungry, but never starving. By being physically hungry, we naturally remain mentally and spiritually hungry. One should never be satisfied with life. Many times I have heard someone say something like, 'Everything in my life was wonderful and then I got cancer and it was such a shock.' If you think you have made it in life or if you think that your life has got as good as it can get, then think again. As spiritual beings we should always be hungry for more learning and a deeper understanding. If you spend most of your time with your stomach full, you mind will become dull and you will be heading for ill health. Since I have understood this simple truth and applied it in my life, I have noticed tremendous changes and insights. Sometimes I am asked how I can have learnt so much in my life. The answer is by being hungry. When I was at school, I had no desire or hunger for learning. I would revise for exams a few weeks before, sit the exam and promptly forget everything the next day. Since I have become hungry for happiness, health and fulfilment, I have found it easy to accumulate a great deal of understanding because I have learnt that physical hunger enhances mental and spiritual hunger.

Another thing that would have astounded the Celts about us is our addiction to water and fluids. The mind and body are intrinsically linked. If you want your mind to be a sponge for knowledge, don't fill your body with excessive water. Common sense dictates that you should only drink when you are thirsty and only as much as it takes to quench your thirst. That is how all animals govern their fluid intake. The current idea of drinking three to five pints (about 2 to 3 litres) of water a day goes against Nature. If we were meant to drink such vast amounts of fluid, we would have an equivalent thirst for it. If you eat in harmony with the season and climate and listen to your body, you will be amazed at how little you need to drink. My eleven-year-old daughter, Lara, drinks four sips of water a week in the middle of winter. She gets all her hydration from her food because her diet consists of porridge (70 per cent water), rice (70 per cent water when cooked) and vegetables, which are all full of fluid. She never shows signs of dehydration and since she has chosen to eat this way has never manifested an illness more serious than a cold.

To the Celts nutrition was about honour and respect both for oneself and for creation. The Celts had a personal relationship with the land and all that grew or grazed upon it. They regarded all creation as sacred and so eating a humble vegetable was as significant as eating a banquet. The land was honoured in the seasonal festivals and the plants were tended with love and respect. They understood that if food was grown, harvested and prepared with honour and respect, it would provide good nourishment. They also understood that if the land was exploited and the plants were starved of the human touch, they would yield little benefit and goodness.

The relationship between humans and the plants that feed us begins with the sowing of the seed. The relationship grows as the seedling is tended and nurtured. As the plant matures, it is given extra attention thus strengthening the bond between plant and man. When the plant is harvested, it gives back to the giver all the love and energy it has taken and so the cycle begins again. Each phase of the cycle is empowered through ceremony and the honouring of creation. It may seem strange, but communicating with and honouring plants increases their yield and the quality of the nutrition they provide.

Our modern approach to farming is one based upon greed and exploitation. It shows little respect for the land and the animals that graze upon it. To the Celts this would seem primitive and unenlightened behaviour. When we read that the Celts sacrificed animals at festival times, we tend to think of an image of the wasteful killing of animals to appease pagan gods. In truth the killing of animals was regarded with great reverence by the Celts and was a relatively rare occurrence compared to the wanton slaughter that goes on every day in the abattoirs of our 'civilised' world. For the Celts to kill any animal was a sacrifice that demanded ceremony to honour the spirit of the animal. When an animal was killed, it gave of its energy and wisdom. Each cell of an animal contains a genetic blueprint of that animal in the DNA and when a human eats that animal, it takes a part of the animal's energy into itself. The Celts knew nothing of DNA but they clearly understood the transfer of energy that takes place. Our senses have become so dulled today that most people are aware of none of this.

In Celtic times animals roamed free and ate from the land. They were not fed anti-biotics, hormones or any other synthetic chemicals. Furthermore they were killed humanely and swiftly. The Celts were skilled hunters and an animal was often not even aware of its impending death. One moment it would be grazing peacefully and the next it would be dead. At the moment of death, the animal would be at peace with the world and at one with creation. Today animals are bred for profit. Over the past fifty years the average life expectancy of a dairy cow has reduced from thirty years to six years. Animals of all kinds are confined in cramped conditions and sent to centres of extermination. When the Nazi's treated the Jews in this way it was rightly regarded as an evil atrocity, yet we treat the rest of creation in exactly the same way every day. As a cow or sheep is driven to an abattoir it can smell death in the air long before it enters the compound. As it is hung upside down by one leg on a conveyor belt its mind is full of fear, pain, anger and confusion. Adrenaline and other hormones pump through its veins and arteries and at the height of its terror, it is killed. All those negative emotions are held within each cut of meat. It is no wonder that, as our consumption of meat has increased, so has violent crime and aggressive behaviour.

The path to true happiness, health and fulfilment must include healthy and responsible eating. Anyone who believes that they can eat anything they like and 'get away with it' is fooling their true self. Sooner or later bad eating habits catch up with you. Many people now regard illness as an occupational hazard of modern living. The truth is that illness only manifests in the bodies of unhealthy individuals and the greatest daily influence upon the health of both mind and body is food.

The power and purity of food

If you want a more spiritual and empowered life, if you want to experience a true connection with Nature, you must change the way you view food. You must stop listening to the voice of advertisers and government-employed health officials and start listening to your own intuition and common sense. It makes no sense to

eat meat that has come from an animal cruelly treated and dis-
honourably slaughtered. Not only are you dishonouring the
animal, but also your own body.

Does it make sense to drink milk products when no other
animal in creation does? If milk really is a good source of calcium,
why is the incidence of osteoporosis ever rising? Scientists have
conducted experiments giving a baby calf its mother's milk but
pasteurising it first. The calf died within weeks from malnutrition.
If a calf cannot get adequate nutrition from its mother's pasteurised
milk, how can humans? The sea is essential for life and yet we fill
it full of waste. Shellfish, the scavengers of the sea, are now so full
of toxins that they are indigestible for many people. Processes
such as hydrogenation used to make spreads more spreadable
release free radicals into the body that act like magnets to attract
and render many nutrients inert and indigestible. Our taste buds
are assaulted with thousands of flavours and sweeteners that con-
fuse both mind and body. It is no coincidence that the rise in
illnesses such as cancer, diabetes, asthma, eczema and ME can be
directly related to the rise in consumption of highly flavoured
convenience foods. If you want to understand the universe you
must simplify your thinking — this can only be achieved if you
simplify your diet. The body cannot understand the language of
artificial additives and preservatives. Nor can it truly understand
synthetic drugs and medications.

The time has come to return to a more simple and respectful
way of living and eating. A way which is in harmony with the
ever-unfolding cycle of creation that whirls around us season by
season. If mankind could understand this simple truth, the world
would be a very different place.

If you want to know how to eat a balanced diet, let Nature teach
you. First of all let us look at ourselves. Human beings have a
mouth with teeth that are primarily used for cutting and grinding
up food. We have three main types of teeth: incisors for cutting
through vegetables, canines for tearing flesh and molars for grinding grains. Grains, meat and vegetables have formed the staple diet
for most humans for thousands of years, but the ratios of different

foods has changed dramatically in recent times. Many people eat meat every day, usually served with vegetables and occasional grains. Others eat only convenience foods that are soft and require little chewing and are composed of highly processed vegetables, meat or grains. This is not how we were designed to eat.

Out of the thirty-two teeth that an adult human possesses, only four are canine teeth designed for meat eating. If meat makes up more than one-eighth (four canines/thirty-two teeth) of your diet, then you are eating far too much. If you look at the ratio of teeth, you can easily see what foods you should be eating and in what proportions. We have twenty molars, four canines and eight incisors, equating to the following food ratios:

Grains	five-eighths	(20/32)
Meat	one-eighth	(4/32)
Vegetables	two-eighths	(8/32)

Eating meat was a rarity for our ancestors, not the norm. It was reserved for special occasions and times when food was scarce. Grains were the staple food of the Celts combined with local vegetables and the occasional meat of which a majority would be fish or fowl. Animals such as boar, deer, bison and sheep were all regarded as sacred and only to be consumed on rare occasions and then only with great ceremony and honouring.

Food was regarded not only as physical nourishment, but as spiritual nourishment too. Preparation of food was always done with thought and reverence because the Celts understood that your state of mind whilst you prepare food affects the quality of the meal. Food cooked with anger will never nourish as well as food cooked with love. The Celts cooked food with intent, which means that they consciously put healing and loving thoughts into their cooking because the nourishment of the tribe was of prime importance. If the tribe were not nourished properly, they would not survive.

The idea of putting love and beautiful thoughts into our food is something we have all experienced. We have all met people who have a natural ability to create delicious food from the simplest of ingredients. They consciously or unconsciously have the ability to put love into their cooking. We have also met people who cannot boil an egg without burning it! These people are not bad cooks, they just do not understand how to cook. Cooking is a magical healing ceremony that, when done correctly, can lift the spirits, rejuvenate the body and inspire the mind. Whenever I cook for others I spend a few minutes thinking about the people I'm cooking for. If we have guests, I spend some time before cooking sitting with them and sensing their needs. If I sense sadness, I fill my mind with joyful thoughts whilst cooking. If I feel tiredness, I think of warmth and relaxation. Your frame of mind has a marked effect upon everything you touch, especially food. Once you understand the power of what I call spiritual cooking, you can have a powerful and positive effect upon everyone you feed.

Eating a balanced diet

It is not easy to simplify your diet. Our taste buds are so used to highly flavoured foods that they have become desensitised to the taste of real food. If you are planning to change your diet, you should be prepared for several weeks of adjustment. You will need to change the way you think about food and the manner in which you prepare it. To gain true nourishment from food requires your mind to 'connect' with the food and be open to accepting the teaching that foods have to give. One of the most ancient ceremonies for doing this is to give thanks for the food and to bless it before you eat it. This pre-dates Christianity by thousands of years and is a practice that many people have sadly rejected because they think it is 'religious'. It is not. It is a spiritual practice that our ancestors understood was important for proper nourishment.

I spoke earlier about the important relationship between man and plant. It is a relationship that has been lost in modern farming practices. Thankfully organic farming is redressing the balance. Organic farming is labour intensive. It requires the farmer to be interacting with his plants on a frequent basis and to always be seeking ways to make the life of the plant as harmonious as possible. In the modern world, especially if you do not have a garden, eating organic foods will be the closest you can get to how our ancestors interacted with and honoured plants. If you are going to eat a plant, surely it deserves to be treated with the utmost care. If you do not eat unadulterated, wholesome food that has been grown with honour and respect for the land, you are transferring that disrespect to your own body. If you do not value your food, you do not value yourself.

Organic foods are more expensive than mass-produced foods, but they should be. If you have a choice between spending 20 per cent of your budget on cheap foods or 80 per cent of your budget on organic foods, many people choose the cheaper option or compromise by spending 50 per cent of their budget on foods some of which are organic. If you compromise your nutrition, you compromise your life. In fact, eating organic does not have to be more costly if you learn the value of eating simply. Furthermore, as your taste buds become more sensitive, you will begin to find 'normal' foods over-flavoured and over-complicated. You will gain more satisfaction and nourishment from a bowl of rice and vegetables than you would from a sumptuous three-course meal. This can only become reality if you stop looking for food to make you feel better and start eating with respect for yourself and creation.

Stimulants like sugar, tea and coffee all give you a quick energy boost, but this is always followed by an equal and opposite energy deficiency which usually requires another boost. Stimulants like these should never be consumed on a daily basis; once or twice a year is perhaps more appropriate. The body of a caffeine addict is in a state of permanent turmoil see-sawing between the highs and lows of energy. This in turn affects the mind and prevents the mental calmness required for us to learn from creation. All stimulants like sugar, caffeine and alcohol rob people of their access to spiritual wisdom. They take the mind and body away from the place of balance and harmony that we all seek.

The staple of a balanced diet should be grains. They are full of vitamins and minerals and provide a steady release of energy. Some plants have energies that are highly developed and contain deep and ancient wisdoms. These plants are called 'master elementals'. They can be regarded as the professors of the plant kingdom with many lessons to teach and insights to impart. Each plant has its own elemental energy or spirit and this will be discussed in more detail in the next chapter.

The most universally available and perhaps the most ancient of grains is rice. It has been nourishing humans for many millennia and can be grown in most climates. By rice I do not mean the polished and highly processed white rice that is available throughout the western world, I mean organic brown rice. In temperate and sub-tropical climates the short-grain variety is what naturally grows and in more tropical climates it is long grain. I regard rice as a master elemental. Brown rice has been my greatest teacher. It has given me a true understanding of the nature of food and this has enabled me to better understand my own nature.

Brown rice, when eaten boiled, will give you virtually all the vitamins and minerals you need. What it will not give you is a false high and neither will it make you feel comforted like a cream cake will. It does not possess the 'feel-good factor' that many modern foods do and is therefore not addictive. What it will do is ground you by giving you a true connection with creation. The energy of brown rice has worked with humans since the dawn of humankind and it understands how to help us on our spiritual journey. We think of rice as being an eastern food, but it is grown in Europe and throughout the world. The east is still famous for its deep spiritual tradition and perhaps part of the reason for that is that their staple food is rice.

The idea of a plant having an energy that can impart deep wisdoms to us is very strange and alien to most westerners. However, if you go and talk to any tribe, anywhere in the world, that eats in harmony with the land and honours creation in ceremony and ritual, you will find that they understand this concept completely. Our ancestors too understood this but we have lost this connection and with it part of our access to spiritual wisdom. To reclaim this understanding we need to look at how our ancestors lived. Fundamental to this is simple living and simple eating.

How to eat simply

If you want to learn how to eat simply you must first understand that any path of long-term restriction is not a healthy path. We are naturally expressive creatures and should not restrict ourselves to such an extent that it causes us to become overly rigid. Having said that, it usually takes a good twelve months of simple eating to discover its true benefits. This allows the body enough time to teach you how to find a good level of balance and harmony in your nutrition. You should then have an understanding of what it feels like to be balanced and so when you do eat more complex foods that have the potential to unbalance you, you know how to get yourself back to a place of harmony quickly and efficiently. If you are suffering from any major illness, it can take longer for you to find balance and harmony, especially if you are on high doses of medication, but with patience and perseverance, it is achievable.

If you choose to eat simply, there are many foods that should be avoided, especially during the first year. Red meat takes between two to four days to digest and unless it comes from a reliable organic source and is killed humanely should never be eaten. If you are a red meat addict, try bison meat instead. It has a similar quality to red meat but is easier to digest and lower in cholesterol than chicken or fish. Shellfish, as we have already seen, should be avoided because of the high level of pollution in the seas. Eating white fish is a much safer option, as these fish tend to inhabit deeper and cleaner waters.

There are also many additives and flavourings, both natural and artificial that have little or no nutritional value and should therefore be avoided. These include flavour enhancers, table salt, pepper, vinegars, spices and E-numbers. Salt (sodium chloride) is essential for life but most westerners have far too much in their diets. There is natural sodium in most foods and if you do add any salt to your food, it should be sea-salt and in the strictest of moderation (once or twice a week would be best and certainly not with every meal). Sugar, especially refined sugar, and artificial sweeteners should also be avoided. Refined sugar is bad for all humans and if you have any illness you should also avoid natural sweeteners such as honey, malts and syrups as they all create acidity within the body. Tomatoes, peppers, aubergine and potatoes are all acidic and should be avoided, especially if you suffer from acid indigestion, irritable bowel syndrome or arthritis. If you are healthy your body can cope with one or two medium-sized baked potatoes per week but this should be a maximum.

Dairy products, especially from pasteurised cow's milk, should not be consumed at all. A little occasional goat's or ewe's cheese is permissible providing you are healthy, but all other milk products should be avoided. This includes butter, yoghurt, cheese, ice cream, casein, whey and lactose. Deep-fried foods should be excluded, as should processed foods and anything containing artificial additives or preservatives. Yeast and fermented foods should be avoided if you suffer from candida albicans, thrush or athlete's foot, as these are all illnesses caused by yeast growth within the body. Finally, social drinking should be kept under strict control. One should judge fluid intake by the amount of fluid output from the body via the bladder. A healthy adult male should urinate no more than three or four times a day and a healthy adult female two or three times a day. Social drinking does not occur in Nature and serves only to overwork the digestive system and kidneys.

A simple, balanced diet should revolve primarily around organic grains and vegetables. What you put into your system first thing in the morning dictates your biochemistry for the day. If you begin your day with a stimulant, such as tea, coffee or sugar (including sugary cereals), you over-stress your body when it is still trying to wake up and this is not healthy. Many of the Celts started their day with porridge made with oats and spring water and it wasn't until I had tried doing this for a year that I began to understand its true benefits. If you start your day by eating a simple grain without added flavour, it has a grounding and energising effect upon the body. It sets you up for the day with an immediate connection to creation that your mind and body can simply understand. Once you add salt, sugar, milk, dried fruit or other ingredients to the porridge, you lose that simple connection.

As with the rice, porridge made with oats and filtered or spring water will do nothing to raise your spirits in the way that sugary drinks or cereals do. But once your mind stops searching for these false 'highs', you will find it hard not to start the day in this way. From a modern nutritional standpoint, starting your day with porridge fills your body with alkalinity, which in a world full of acid-forming foods and acid-creating stress is highly beneficial. Your body will love it, but the chances are your ego will hate it. It offers little taste until your taste buds adjust and this is not how we expect food to be. But once your body has adjusted to the taste, which takes only a few weeks, the porridge begins to taste naturally sweet and full of flavour.

The main grain consumed with other meals should be organic brown rice. There are a variety of other healthy grains that can be cooked including couscous, millet, bulgar wheat and buckwheat. Other grains such as corn, wheat, barley and rye can be consumed in the form of bread (note: wheat and rye contain high levels of gluten which some people are intolerant to) or crackers. These grains can be combined with fresh, organic seasonal vegetables, which can be steamed, stir-fried or cooked in a casserole. In a temperate climate vegetables available will, depending on the time of year, include carrots, onions, garlic, parsnip, swede, turnip, celeriac, celery, spring onions, radish, watercress, cauliflower, leeks, cabbage, runner beans, French beans, broad beans, sprouts, squash and sea vegetables such as kelp and Japanese seaweeds.

These foods can be supplemented with beans and pulses (sprouted or cooked), seeds (sunflower, sesame, pumpkin) and a little white meat (chicken or turkey) or deep-sea fish (cod, haddock, tuna, plaice, for example). If you are vegetarian there are non-animal sources of protein, including soya products such as tofu, but protein should make up no more that 10 per cent of your dietary intake. If you are fit and healthy you may also have a little seasonal fruit, which in winter in a temperate climate consists of apples and pears only. However, if you are ill or overweight, such foods should be avoided until you are healthy. You can also use an organic, non-hydrogenated spread on your bread and cold-pressed corn or sesame oil to cook with as these two oils do not form hard to digest saturated chains when they are cooked once. Finally, fluid intake should be kept to a minimum and should be governed by thirst.

If you adopt this way of eating, you may well feel terrible in the first few weeks as your body adjusts to the new foods and clears out all the toxins you have accumulated over the years. But if you persist you will find amazing changes in your energy levels and your state of mind. You will begin to perceive the subtle energies of creation and start to see the world around you in a new light. The quality of your skin, eyes, hair and nails will improve as your body begins the process of rejuvenation that naturally occurs when you eat in this way. I have found that changing my way of eating has been the biggest single influence on my spiritual development. I was horrified when it was first suggested that I eat porridge made with water, but now I have learnt to like it, I rarely start my day any other way, even in the height of summer.

You should be warned however that changing your diet is a big decision and one that will only reap benefits if adhered to completely. If you eat simply during the week and binge at weekends you will make yourself very ill. Your body will love the simple food and hate the complex food and is likely to let you know this by giving you symptoms of sickness and/or diarrhoea. This is not a fancy health diet that can be 'played with' but a serious life choice that should only be undertaken if you are committed to trying to find balance and harmony in your life.

All food should ideally be prepared and cooked using natural utensils such as wood or stainless steel and on a non-electric heat source. It should also be cooked and consumed in an atmosphere or love and tranquillity. If you are in a bad mood you should neither cook nor eat until you have changed your headspace. If you cook with stress, you will eat with stress and this will weaken your immune system and unbalance you. Food should be prepared with honour and respect, which means with care and attention. Fast and convenience eating is not the domain of the spiritual being and will never lead to balance and harmony.

How you eat your food also has a marked effect on how well or poorly it nourishes you. Food should be consumed with thought and respect for creation that provided it and for yourself. Eating on the run or bolting food down is neither healthy nor respectful. In the orient 200 chews per mouthful is recommended although most westerners find it difficult to manage fifty chews per mouthful. Chewing is an essential part of digestion. The salivary glands produce enzymes that help to break down our food. If you chew your food properly you will do 80 per cent of your digestion before you swallow leaving only 20 per cent for your digestive system to do. Most westerners do little more than 20 per cent of their digestion through chewing leaving much more work for the body to do once the food is swallowed. Next time you are at a restaurant check the average number of chews that people make before swallowing. It can be as little as two or three. Giving thanks for food is also important, but this can be done quietly in your mind if it is inappropriate to do so publicly. Before I eat any meal I always try to spend a few moments in quiet thought giving thanks for the food and mentally preparing my body to digest it.

Food should not only be cooked, but also presented, with love. If a meal is attractively presented, just looking at it stimulates the production of digestive juices in the mouth. Once your mind and body are in balance and harmony, as you look at the food on your plate your subconscious mind is already preparing the correct balance of enzymes to perfectly digest the food. The more complex the meal, the harder it is for your body and mind to do this. Finally, drinking whilst eating should be avoided because it dilutes the digestive juices making digestion less efficient. If you chew your food properly you should have no need to drink whilst eating.

The idea of giving up alcohol, sugar, coffee, tea and processed foods in favour of simple eating may seem extreme but from my experience is it the only way to truly find your power and connection to creation. If you adopt a simple diet, you may find yourself suffering from terrible cravings for more complex foods, but this should only serve to reinforce your determination to break free from your addictions and dependencies. It may seem illogical to seek freedom through restriction, but the ultimate aim is to be able to eat and transmute any food. Once you have a true mind and body connection, you can mentally instruct your body to digest anything. If you can achieve this, you will ultimately be able to travel anywhere and eat the local food. How many westerners could then travel to India or Africa and eat what the locals eat without ill effect?

Many people ask me how they can make simple food appetising. The answer is to use the mind and the imagination. A simple meal of rice and stir-fried vegetables and beans if cooked with love and presented with beauty will be both appetising and tasty. I cannot emphasise enough the importance of the mind in the process of food preparation and presentation. Furthermore, when we eat we should be seeking nutrition and sustenance, not complicated flavours and stimulants. In many parts of the world, especially in areas noted for their strong and highly developed spiritual systems, such as India and China, the people eat simple food every day. Often they eat the same meal every day. They have learnt from birth to eat for nourishment and to find happiness and upliftedness with the mind. In the west we have to teach ourselves this way of thinking because we are taught as children to use foods to comfort us and make us feel better. Until we learn to let go of this, we will never find our spiritual inheritance.

There are many different and tasty meals that can be made with simple foods if you feel the need for variety in your diet. You can make salads, soups, sandwiches, stews, vegetable spreads, casseroles and a whole host of other delicious recipes. If you need inspiration, find any recipe and adapt it to your simple diet. Take out all unnecessary flavouring and substitute non-seasonal vegetables with seasonal ones. If the recipe uses tomatoes, try substituting grated pumpkin or carrot. If you need stock, make your own by boiling up the tops of vegetables and so on. All it takes is a little inventiveness and imagination.

The power of fasting

Throughout the world, amongst many different spiritual traditions, fasting plays an important role in spiritual development. If life is difficult or you are going through a time of transition, simplifying your thinking and initiating change are two important keys to allowing the process to unfold. Fasting activates both these keys quickly and efficiently and is potentially very powerful. Because fasting has the power to bring about great good, it also has an equal and opposite power to do harm if not carried out with thought, understanding and preparation. To go without food for a day is achievable by most people, but fasting for longer can be potentially dangerous both to physical and mental health if not done correctly.

When you fast, your biochemistry is no longer being bombarded with a wide variety of chemicals to analyse and process. This allows it to function much more simply, which in turn makes your thinking much simpler. Simple does not mean stupid, it means uncomplicated. The answers to all problems are simple, but our complex eating and thinking makes many solutions unreachable. By simplifying your diet through fasting, your thinking becomes simple and with it can come clear perceptions of how to move forward in any situation. Whenever you feel 'stuck' the answer is to initiate change and fasting is one of the best methods for doing this.

To go without food or drink for an extended time can be dangerous. A much safer, but still beneficial way to fast is to eat only one type of food. Ideally this food should contain all the vitamins and minerals you need and the best food for this is brown rice. You can safely fast by just eating brown rice and drinking a little filtered or spring water for up to ten days if your body has already cleaned out toxins through the simple eating plan laid out above. Be warned though that going from a western diet straight into fasting will make you ill and could do your mind and body serious damage. Rice fasting releases toxins from the body at a deep level and if you have not cleared your body of the toxins circulating every day in your blood, you can become overloaded with toxins once the rice fast begins to release the deeper toxins.

Whenever we have emotional trauma, the body seeks to release negative emotions because they are not conducive to health and well-being. If the body is busy trying to balance itself due to complex eating, it cannot always release the emotion and so it seeks to store it. Also sometimes we hold on to the emotion in our minds and this creates a subconscious message for the body to store the emotion. The body does this by taking toxins from our food, burying the emotion in the toxins and then burying the toxins deep in the body tissue. Rice fasting allows these toxins to be released and the negative emotions that are stored within them. This can give rise to feelings of hurt, anger, resentment and so on, but once you understand that this is just the release of negative emotions from the past, you can mentally let them go. Many people who try fasting do not realise this and, when the negative emotions arise, they subconsciously hold on to them, which means they just get buried again within the body.

Fasting on rice can bring tremendous inspiration and insight. One of the reasons I regard rice as a master elemental is because it has taught me so much. When you fast on rice, each day brings new understandings and enlightenments. You feel yourself becoming cleaner and clearer in body, mind and spirit. Your senses become highly tuned and you begin to perceive your spiritual path with clarity. It is best to start with a short fast of two or three days before embarking on longer fasts. How you prepare for a period of fasting is very important. Firstly you should have been eating simply for at least six months prior to fasting for the first time. In the days leading up to the fast you should cut all protein out of your diet, including meat, fish and beans. It is also good to simplify your life as much as possible prior to fasting so that your focus is not affected. Make sure you will not have to pay bills or write letters, for example, whilst you are fasting as this will detract from the insights that come with it. You may even like to perform a simple ceremony the night before you start to set out your intent and focus your thoughts.

How you come out of the other side of fasting is also very important. Many people eat all sorts of different foods immediately after fasting to 'make up' for the foods they have missed. This over-stresses the body and if you are not healthy can be very dangerous. The day after finishing a fast should be started simply with porridge (organic oats and filtered or spring water only). The rest of the day you should then stick to plain rice. The second day you can introduce a few seasonal vegetables and from then on slowly work your way back to the simple eating laid out earlier in this chapter. Animal protein (if you are not vegetarian) should be the last thing you introduce. The slower you broaden your diet again, the better. Finally, if you are suffering from any serious illness, you are best advised to fast under the supervision of a qualified and experienced practitioner.

Communicating with illness

Eating a simple diet will provide improvement to virtually any illness, but if you learn to communicate with your illness, you will also find a cure. All illness is your body's way of telling you that you are out of balance. If you learn to communicate with your illness, it will tell you how to restore balance and harmony in your life because that is its purpose. All illness comes to teach and instruct us. Once you have learnt everything an illness has to teach you, it will cease to exist in your life. The problem is that in the west we are taught that illness is our enemy and it should be fought with drugs or surgery. If neither is appropriate then you are 'incurable'. All the time you try to fight an illness, you compound it by feeding it energy. Once you learn to embrace your illness and regard it as a friend, not a foe, you will be much further along the road to recovery.

As you simplify your diet, spend time meditating on what your body and illness are trying to show you. The body manifests illnesses in areas of our lives that need attention. If you have an eye problem, you are not seeing something in your life with clarity and perspective. If you have ear problems, you are not listening to something. If you have illness in a major organ, look at the related element and see if you are lacking the resources that element has to offer. For instance, the illness of the lungs relates to unlearnt lessons, whereas illness of the kidneys relates to a lack of power and groundedness. Illness of the heart relates to a lack of joy and upliftedness in your life and illness of the liver relates to a lack of expression. There is no such thing as an incurable disease, only a lack of understanding as to where the cure lies. Your illness is like a series of questions to which you have to find answers. If you search with hunger and determination, there is nothing that cannot be overcome.

Five

CELTIC TREE MEDICINE

The Celts regarded everything in creation as part of an inter-connected web of energy and this meant that all things in creation were related. Plants, trees, animals, stones and all heavenly bodies were thought of as brothers, sisters, parents or grandparents. They also regarded every individual part of creation as having its own unique energy or 'spirit' that could be communicated with and learnt from. This was not superstition, rather, a deep and profound understanding of the nature of the universe. The Celts, like many other indigenous peoples throughout the world, held the belief that each plant has an elemental energy that could be contacted and communicated with just as we communicate with one another.

My first experience of this was as a young boy. When I was seven years old my parents took my older brothers and me to a fête that was taking place at my brothers' school. There were various stalls selling toys and cakes but I was drawn to a stall selling plants. I had already developed a keen interest in gardening from spending time with my father at his allotment where he grew many of our family's vegetables. I was fascinated by the whole process of working with plants and had witnessed the time and care required to make crops grow successfully. On this stall there were various herbs and houseplants, but most were out of the price range of a small boy with only sixpence pocket money. At the front of the table was a baby spider plant in a paper cup and for some reason it called out to me. I didn't hear it speak in my mind, I just felt a sense that it wanted to come home with me.

I asked how much it was and was told it was sixpence. I asked my father if I could buy it and he explained that, if I bought it, it would use up all of my money and, if I saw anything else I liked on another stall, I would not be able to buy it. I was undeterred and using all the passion and determination I could muster pleaded to be allowed to buy it. Seeing that I had clearly made up my mind, my father allowed me to buy it and I proudly carried it home. As the weeks and months went by, I tended my plant with love and it responded by growing ever larger. I had to regularly transplant it into a larger pot and when it was fully grown it began to sprout baby plants. I was enthralled by this wonder of creation and was soon transplanting the baby plants into individual pots.

It didn't take long before we were overrun with spider plants. The babies had babies and soon I was giving away these plants to friends and neighbours. My parents and I still have offspring originating from that one small plant and we are still giving away baby plants over thirty years later. I have long lost track of all the offspring I have given away but I am sure that the original plant now has thousands of direct descendants dotted all over the country and even perhaps in other countries. This is the miracle of creation and from the moment that first plant called out to me I was fascinated by it. You may think that it was little more than a childhood whim but I can still remember that one plant, out of all the plants on the table, clearly calling to me with its energy. I cannot truly explain it but the fact that it still remains clear in my mind after all these years tells me that the experience was real and significant in my life.

Since then, as I have searched and studied more, I have gained a deep respect and understanding of the concept of plant energies and have formed personal relationships with many plants and trees over the years. If you talk to anyone who has worked with growing plants over many years, they will tell you that they have become attached to some plants. It may be a plant that needed nursing back to health after attack by disease or it may be that it has taken years of love and attention to reach maturity, but there is a connection that makes the plant more than just a plant. This is the first step towards understanding and communicating with plants. Plants are much more than pretty or functional vegetation.

They have a spirit, a consciousness, that can be communicated with and learnt from.

With our modern farming practices we have lost touch with the energies of plants. We have become distanced from them and no longer understand their importance in the web of creation. To the Celts plants provided food, medicine, insight and inspiration. Out of all the plants, the Celts regarded trees as particularly sacred. Each tree provided its own teachings and healing as well as materials for tools, weapons, housing, fencing and dyes. Because of their respect for creation, trees were never merely chopped down for use. Any tree that gave of itself was honoured with ceremony and offerings. If a tree was to give of its fruit, sap or bark then it would be interacted with and honoured throughout its growth. If it were to give of itself in entirety, for building, for example, then permission would be asked of it before it was felled and, once taken, every part of the tree would be utilised.

I was asked by a local farmer some years ago to fell an ash tree on his land. He said that it needed to be felled, as it was on land where he was building and that if I felled it I could use all the wood. If I had owned the land I would have left the tree where it was, but it was not my land. The tree was going to be felled anyway so I felt that it would be better if I did it with honour and respect than if it were merely cut down by someone else. I spent four days communicating with the tree with prior to felling it. I told it that the farmer had asked me to fell it but that if it would allow me, I would honour it with ceremony and by utilising its wood with respect. I explained to it mentally that it needed to send its energy back into the earth because I was going to cut it down and that it should have no fear — its energy would live on.

The next day I went with my friend Eli to cut it down. Before I began, I once more connected with the tree by placing my hand on it. As I touched the tree, a clear picture came into my mind of how and where to cut it. It was as if the tree understood its destiny, was willingly accepting it and at the same time informing me how best to cut it down. After a simple ceremony I started my chainsaw and began to cut as I had been instructed. When the saw first cut I felt a moment of fear from the tree followed immediately by total acceptance. The tree fell perfectly in precisely the place I needed it to with a grace and beauty beyond description. It was like a hound obediently lying down for its master.

The wood from the tree was used in many different ways. I cut a staff for Eli from it and made a love-seat for our garden along with a table to go in front of it. Some of the wood was used in our ceremonial fires and some to heat our home during the winter. Virtually every part of the tree was used and its life is still honoured each time Debbie and I sit on the seat together or Eli takes his staff out for a walk. The table has now become an altar on which we make offerings when doing ceremony and each time it is used I feel a connection to the energy of that ash tree. This is just one of many magical encounters I have had with trees. I mentally talk with them whenever I meet them and they talk back to me, sometimes in words that form in my mind and sometimes in images and pictures.

This may appear to be the behaviour of a madman but it is how our ancestors lived every day of their lives. I am now so used to it that to me it is normal and certainly much more than the work of an overactive imagination.

I have even had trees call out to me to come and meet them. I remember coming to the end of a long walk one sunny afternoon when a yew tree called out to me. I was walking along a woodland path when into my mind came the words, 'Hey, come up here.' I looked up and saw a yew tree standing about 50 metres up a steep bank. 'Come up here,' it said again, 'I have something to show you.' 'But I'm tired,' I replied. 'Are you sure I need to see you today?' The tree was very insistent so I began to climb the bank. I expected to perhaps find a feather or an animal bone so when I reached the top I made physical contact with the tree to say 'Hello' and then looked around on the ground, but could see nothing. 'Look up,' the tree said, so I looked up and saw a tall, straight branch that was perfect for a staff. I had been looking for a yew staff for some months but up until then had not found one. I asked the tree if this was why it had called to me and it said 'yes' and told me that I could harvest it at Beltane, which was the next festival. On the morning of Beltane I walked down and, after leaving an offering of a horseshoe I found on the way and performing a simple ceremony, I climbed up and cut the branch. It is now seasoning in my garage and when I am called to I will carve and decorate it. This is the magic of trees and a reality in my life as it was in the lives of the Celts.

The ogham

The ogham (pronounced *OH-wahm* or *OH-gahm*) was a unique Celtic alphabet used by the Druids for divination, magic, secret communication and inscriptions. It originated in Britain perhaps as early as 2200 BCE (before common era) where nearly all surviving examples are to be found. Most of these are inscriptions on memorial stones. Much of today's information about the ogham comes from a fifteenth-century manuscript called *The Book of Ballymote* which was probably transcribed from more ancient texts. In it are described the origins of the ogham as follows:

> From whence, what time and what person, and from what cause did the ogham spring? The place is Hybernia's Isle, which we Scots inhabit; in a time of Breass, the son of Elathan, then king of all Ireland. The person was Ogma MacElathan, the son of Dealbadh, brother to Breass; for Breass, Ogma and Dealbadh were the three sons of Elathan, who was the son of Dealbath. Ogma, being a man such skilled in dialects and in poetry, it was he who invented ogham, its objects being signs of secret speech known only to the learned, and designed to be kept from the vulgar and poor of the nation ... On a Birch it was written and given to Lugh, the son of Etlem ...

Unlike most other alphabets, the ogham does not have separ-ate, unique characters but sets of five letters represented by one, two, three, four or five lines above, below or bisecting a base line called a **druim**. On standing stones the corner of the stone formed the druim and was known as the **arris**. The ogham letters were called **fedha** or **fews** and were written either from left to right or top to bottom with inscriptions often starting with a symbol called a 'feather' (>). There were originally four sets of five fews although another set of signs was added later to represent diphthongs. The twenty original fews were as follows:

> B L F S N H D T C Q M G Ng St R A O U E I

To the Celts, the written word was considered so powerful that it was a rarity rather than the norm. The whole Celtic language at that time was full of connections and meanings that were so deep and complex we may never know their true significance. The Celts believed that words beginning with the same letter were symbol-ically and magically connected so that each letter represented a tree, colour, bird, profession and a whole host of other meanings that have been lost over time. Some trees are not trees at all but plants — clearly the Celtic definition a what a tree was differs from the modern view. The name of each letter represented a tree as shown in the table.

To understand the symbolic meaning of each tree we need to look at how the Celts utilised each tree and what they associated with them. Most meanings arise from simple observation of the nature and practical uses of trees combined with known Celtic magical associations. It is not always clear how the corresponding bird and colour fit into the symbolism but I have included details of these for each ogham along with what I have discovered of their significance and symbolism. Some colours such as 'fiery' and 'thorn' are more obscure in what they represent and I suspect that these colours were perhaps only seen in the Otherworld. Each tree, bird and colour is written first with its Celtic name followed by its English translation. I have also included each ogham's numerological value for those who study numerology.

Ogham	Letter	Name	Pronunciation	Tree (*Botanical name*)
B	b	beth	*BEH*	Birch (*Betula pendula*)
L	l	luis	*LWEESH*	Rowan (*Sorbus aucuparia*)
F	f	fearn	*FAIR-n*	Alder (*Alnus glutinosa*)
S	s	saille	*SAHL-yuh*	Willow (*Salix spp.*)
N	n	nion	*NEE-uhn*	Ash (*Fraxinus excelsior*)
H	h	huath	*HOO-ah*	Hawthorn (*Crataegus monogyna*)
D	d	duir	*DOO-r*	Oak (*Quercus robur*)
T	t	tinne	*CHIN-yuh*	Holly (*Ilex aquifolia*)
C	c	coll	*CULL*	Hazel (*Corylus avellana*)
Q	q	quert	*KWAIRT*	Apple (*Malus sylvestris*)
M	m	muin	*MUHN*	Bramble (*Rubus fruticosa*)
G	g	gort	*GORT*	Ivy (*Hedera helix*)
Ng	ng	ngetal	*NYEH-tl*	Reed (*Phragmites*)
St	st	straiff	*STRAHF*	Blackthorn (*Prunus spinosa*)
R	r	ruis	*RWEESH*	Elder (*Sambucus nigra*)
A	a	ailm	*AHL-m*	Elm (*Ulmus procera*)
O	o	onn	*UHN*	Gorse (*Ulex europaeus*)
U	u	ur	*OO-rah*	Heather (*Calluna vulgaris*)
E	e	eadha	*EH-yuh*	Aspen (*Populus tremula*)
I	i	iubhar	*EE-yah*	Yew (*Taxus baccata*)

Beth

Letter: B

Tree: Beth — Birch

Bird: Besan — Pheasant

Colour: Ban — White

Original meaning: Mother goddess; purification; renewal

Numerological value: 8

The birch had a multitude of uses, practically, medically and magically, for the Celts. Birch wood was used for making cradles, roofs and boats whilst its sap was used as a sweetener and for making wine and vinegar. Its bark was used for writing on and making ale and it also yielded an oil that was used for tanning hides. Medicinally, the bark and leaves were used to treat kidney problems, rheumatism, fevers, skin disorders and urinary infections. Symbolically it has long associations with cleansing, purification, protection and fertility. The first ogham was written on a switch of birch and brooms were made from its twigs to cleanse homes and sweatlodges. At Samhain the old year was symbolically driven out with a birch broom and the tradition of 'birching' as a punishment for crimes evolved from a Celtic purification ritual where 'evil-spirits' were beaten out of law-breakers using a birch cane. Birch logs with their bark removed were used for Yule logs and the Beltane Maypole was also traditionally made of birch. The Beltane celebrations revolve around a fertility rite and the corresponding ogham bird, the pheasant, also has a long association with fertility.

Luis
Letter: L
Tree: Luis — Rowan
Bird: Lachan — Duck
Colour: Liath — Grey
Original meaning: Flame; protection against psychic attack
Numerological value: 7

The Celts regarded the rowan, or mountain ash as it is sometimes called, as a magical tree that provided physical and psychic protection. It was used to protect against lightning and to ward off enchantment and its bright red berries bear the sign of the *pentagram*, the magical five-pointed star of protection. It was said that only a rowan whip or branch could break the spell of an enchanted horse. A cross made by binding two pieces of rowan together with red thread was used as a protective charm placed above the doors of houses: 'Rowan tree, red thread, holds the witches all in dread' (old English rhyme).

A drink made from rowanberries and incense made from its leaves and fruit were used by shamans to aid visionary journeys and berries or bark were worn on the body as an aid to healing. Both bark and fruit have medicinal value and have been used in the treatment of stomach upsets and kidney disorders. The boiled fruit also makes an excellent gargle for sore throats. Rowan's corresponding bird, the duck, has a long symbolic association with emotional balance and protection.

Fearn

Letter: F
Tree: Fearn — Alder
Bird: Faelinn — Gull
Colour: Flann — Crimson
Original meaning: Blood; fire; freeing the earth from water
Numerological value: 8

The alder is often found growing by streams and in damp places. When its wood comes into contact with water, it turns black and hardens, making it exceedingly durable. The Celts used alder for building boats, bridges and foundations in wet or damp areas. It made excellent charcoal and so was favoured by smiths and its bark and leaves were used medicinally to treat fevers, burns, skin problems, fleas and lice.

To the Celts alder was a fairy tree. When its wood is cut it 'bleeds' turning from white to red and this led its link with Fear Dearg, the Red Man who, according to Celtic legend, helps humans to escape from the land of fairy. It yields three different colours for dyes, brown from its twigs, red from its bark and green from its flowers representing earth, fire and water respectively. The green dye was, according to legend, the colour used to dye fairy clothes. The seagull too has associations with the land of fairy because it inhabits the shoreline, traditionally the magical link between two worlds, that of the land and sea. Shamans were said to imitate the call of the gull to summon up the wind and whistles made from green alder wood were said to do the same.

Saille

Letter: S
Tree: Saille — Willow
Bird: Seg — Hawk
Colour: Sodath — Fiery
Original meaning: Harmony; the moon
Numerological value: 22

The willow tree favours watery places and a cut branch when planted will root and grow into a new tree, hence its association with growth and rebirth. Willow was used in an annual Celtic purification ceremony, which later developed into 'beating the bounds' a ritual used to define the parish boundary each year. Its affinity with water led it to be associated with the moon and willow wands were cut at Full Moon for use in lunar ceremonies. The twigs of a birch broom were traditionally bound using willow thongs to help the negative energies flow more easily during cleansing ceremonies. It was sacred to poets and bards as a tree of inspiration and insight and was the favoured wood used in water divining.

A tea or incense of willow bark was taken to contact the divine feminine as well as for pain relief in the treatment of fevers, mouth disorders and as an external wash for wounds, sores, burns and other skin disorders. Its flexibility also made willow the choice for weaving baskets and making hurdles — the traditional Celtic fencing used in keeping livestock. The hawk's association with willow is unclear although these birds are traditionally said to inspire visions and bring messages. They are also noted for their swiftness and flexibility in flight and powerful grip.

Nion
Letter: N
Tree: Nion — Ash
Bird: Naescu — Snipe
Colour: Necht — Clear
Original meaning: Rebirth; linking the upper and lower worlds
Numerological value: 7

The ash tree represents the *axis mundi* or 'world tree'. In Celtic times it grew especially tall and was seen to have its roots deep within the earth, its trunk in this world and its top branches touching the heavens. This represented the three Celtic worlds — the Underworld or fairy realm, Middle Earth where we normally exist and the heavens or Land of Spirits — in balance and harmony. The symbolism also relates to the integration of past, present and future. To the Celts the spiral buds of the ash represented the spiral of life, as seen on a Druid's ash wand decorated with spirals found on the Isle of Anglesey in Wales.

The ash had strong links with warrior energy. Young warriors were given ash spears to test their ability to hit straight and true as part of their rites of passage into adulthood. The pole of the birch broom was traditionally made of ash as a protection against negativity and the idea of personal protection was also seen in the Celts' use of ash in weapons as spears and in axe handles. An ash leaf placed under a pillow was said to produce prophetic dreams perhaps because the leaves were in touch with the Land of Spirits from where the Celts believed prophecies came.

On a practical level ash wood was used for making oars, carts, tool handles, fencing and furniture. Medicinally, it was used as a mild laxative and diuretic, to regulate the bowels, expel intestinal parasites, reduce fevers and treat kidney and urinary problems.

The ash also has a reputation for attracting lightning which to the Celts was a sign of powerful energies coming to earth from the Land of Spirits. There is an old country saying, 'Ash courts the flash' that confirms this. It is the ash's affinity to lightning that may explain its link with the snipe. The snipe flies in a zigzag pattern said to mimic lightning and its drumming call is said to imitate the roar of the thunder.

Huath

Letter: H
Tree: Huath — Hawthorn
Bird: Hadaig — Nightcrow
Colour: Huath — Thorn
Original meaning: The Crone aspect of the triple goddess; sexuality
Numerological value: 22

The hawthorn is a holy tree often found growing by sacred wells. It was associated with psychic protection, probably because of its sharp thorns, and hawthorn hedges were planted around fields and holy places as a protection against negativity. Fairies were said to inhabit hawthorn groves and were especially drawn to hawthorns growing together with oak and ash trees. In Celtic times the hawthorn was considered so sacred that the felling of it was punishable by death, which gave the tree an unfair reputation in later times as a tree of bad luck. It was also linked with the wild, untamed, feminine side of human nature that is so feared in patriarchal society and this, along with its association with the crow and its link to death, may have exaggerated its negative reputation.

To the Celts the hawthorn was a most magical tree. Its blooming in the spring announced the coming of Beltane with all its associations with fertility and fairy magic. It is a very feminine tree and, in one encounter with a hawthorn tree, I was shown a vision of the guardian spirit or elemental energy of the hawthorn. She appeared to me as a beautiful, tall, pale-skinned young woman with long white hair stretching to the ground. Her hair was not only the longest I had ever seen, it sparkled in the sun and with each sparkle there was the sound of a musical note. I sat transfixed by the magical melody that these sparkling notes played as she danced in the sunshine.

Medicinally, the hawthorn berry treats heart ailments. In modern herbalism it is used to treat both high and low blood pressure, due to the berry's unique biochemistry that contains a chemical that acts as a blood pressure balancer. If your blood pressure is too low it raises it and if it is too high it lowers it. Drug manufacturers have never been able to duplicate this normalising effect.

Duir

Letter: D
Tree: Duir — Oak
Bird: Droen — Wren
Colour: Dub — Black
Original meaning: Door; midsummer; Druid
Numerological value: 7

The oak is one of the most written about trees in Celtic literature. A very durable hardwood, it was much favoured by the Celts and was used for building boats, doors and gates; 'the King of the Forest', it was associated with strength and endurance. The word **duir** means 'door' and to the Celts it was a most sacred tree whose ancient wisdom facilitated going through spiritual doorways into new realms of experience. The Druids held the oak in high esteem as a very magical and powerful tree and they favoured oak groves for performing rituals and ceremony. The oak attracts lightning and an oak struck by lightning was considered particularly powerful. Its wood would be taken for use as a talisman to ward off lightning and for connecting with the energies of the thunder spirits.

The oak was honoured during the midsummer festival and this time was favoured for cutting oak staffs and wands. The word Druid can be translated as 'one having knowledge of the oak' and it was the knowledge of how to decipher the wisdom of the oak that was an important part of the inner or secret teaching of Druidry. Just as the oak was the king of trees, so the Druids regarded its associated bird, the wren, as the king of birds. (The reason why the Druids regarded such a small bird as the king originates from Celtic myth and will be related in the next chapter.) Another interesting thing about the oak is that its roots are said to grow equal in length and size to its branches and so the oak is the living embodiment of 'as above, so below': anything that is done in heaven is mirrored on earth, and vice versa. The Celtic shamans believed that anything that they balanced or healed in the spirit or fairy realm would automatically be mirrored in the physical world.

To prevent damage during a storm, the willow shows strength in weakness by bending in the wind. Although the oak is a very strong and durable tree, in a ferocious storm its strength and rigidity make it weak and vulnerable to cracking or even being uprooted. This teaches the need to temper strength with flexibility.

Medicinally, the oak was used to treat fevers, mouth and throat irritations, skin sores and menstrual problems.

Tinne

Letter: T
Tree: Tinne — Holly
Bird: Truith — Starling
Colour: Temen — Dark grey
Original meaning: Boldness; fire; fatherhood
Numerological value: 8

The holly tree was associated with winter, particularly the winter solstice. Celtic myth tells of the epic battle that is fought every year between the Oak King and the Holly King representing summer and winter respectively. The Holly King is born on the dawn of midsummer's day, the time when the power of the Oak King has reached its peak. During the autumn months the Holly King grows in power and strength whilst the energy of the Oak King wanes. On midwinter's eve the Holly King is crowned and honoured, but the very next day its power is already waning because midwinter's day announces the rebirth of the Oak King. So the epic battle once again gathers momentum towards the next midsummer.

The holly was associated with warrior energy and spear shafts and clubs were often made from its wood, as were chariot wheels. The leaves of the holly begin life soft and pliable but as they age they harden forming an impenetrable barrier and the red berries symbolised fire and sacrificial blood. All these attributes can be linked to those sought by the warrior, flexibility tempered with hardness and the willingness to endure pain and sacrifice. The Druids brought holly sprigs into their dwellings to welcome all tree spirits to their homes during the barren winter months. This was to ensure that the fires throughout the winter using wood from the forest would burn hot and strong. Holly was considered a lucky tree providing protection against poisoning and was used medicinally to treat fevers and rheumatism. The starling is a very sociable bird that teaches us how to live in harmony with those around us — another important attribute for a warrior.

Coll

Letter: C
Tree: Coll — Hazel
Bird: Corr — Crane
Colour: Cron — Brown
Original meaning: Wisdom; divination
Numerological value: 6

The hazel tree appears frequently in Celtic legend and its nuts were said to hold the knowledge of all arts and sciences. One story tells of nine hazel trees dropping nine hazelnuts into a sacred pool. The nuts were then eaten by a salmon, a fish that the Celts regarded as the oldest and wisest of all creatures. The number nine seems to be very closely linked to the hazel and this may this is born out by the fact that it takes nine years of growth before a new hazel tree will bear fruit. Carrying a hazel staff was a sign of authority in Celtic times and hazel wands are still favoured by modern-day magicians. Divining rods for water divining have also traditionally been made from hazel. Its wood was considered to be infused with protective and powerful magic.

Its flexibility when freshly cut during its growing season meant it was favoured for making hurdles and baskets and its nut was not only used in cooking, but also as a treatment for coughs. Its associated bird, the crane, was regarded as guardian to the Celtic

Underworld and associated with the sea god Manannan Mac Lir who had a medicine bag made from crane skin that he filled with magical treasures. The wonderful thing about the hazel is that it grows many straight branches and is not harmed if one or two are cut from it. On the contrary, if the tree has been coppiced it is actually beneficial to the tree to cut away branches. This makes it the perfect tree for novices to work with because they can do little harm and at the same time can learn from this wonderful tree's wisdom. In woodland close to my home there is one very ancient hazel tree that I go to and sit under if I have a problem to solve. The tree always gives me new perspectives and insights.

Quert

Letter. Q
Tree: Quert — Apple
Bird: Querc — Hen
Colour. Quair — Mouse coloured
Original meaning. Eternity; rebirth
Numerological value: 9

In Celtic times **quert** referred to the crab-apple, the ancestor of many modern orchard varieties. It was associated with the feminine-divine, the goddess as she appears in all her many forms, due to the fact that if its fruit is cut, the core reveals the shape of a five-pointed star, which is sacred to the goddess. The Celts associated the number five with the five stages of growth in women, namely birth, initiation, love, repose and death. In Arthurian legend, the Isle of Avalon means 'the isle of apples' and was a mystical island not of this world. It was also linked to the Underworld and the Samhain tradition of apple-bobbing was symbolic of dipping into the Underworld to gain the fruits of wisdom. Cider made from fermented apples was sometimes drunk ceremonially at Samhain to aid journeying to other realms and to inspire visions. If you have ever drunk real scrumpy (traditionally made cider) you may be aware that it can stimulate vivid dreams.

The apple was also symbolic of love and there were many divinatory practices revolving around reading the numbers and patterns of apple pips to discover knowledge about a future lover. Another love divination of more modern times involves peeling an apple and tossing the peel over your shoulder. If the peel forms a letter it is said to be the initial of your next lover. Because of their association with love, apples were also linked to fertility. This may explain its associated bird being the hen because it too is linked with fertility.

Muin

Letter: M
Tree: Muin — Bramble
Bird: Mintan — Titmouse
Colour: Mbracht — Variegated
Original meaning: Gathering; assimilation; learning
Numerological value: 3

In the Irish language the word 'muin' is used to describe any thicket of thorny plants, but it is generally accepted that the bramble is the most likely related tree. Some versions of the ogham link the vine to **muin** which, though cultivated in Britain since Celtic times, is not indigenous to the island. The vine and the bramble share many similarities with both being favoured for making wine and in cooking. Medicinally, blackberries, the fruit of the bramble, were used to treat diarrhoea and dysentery and are an excellent source of vitamin C. The leaves were used to treat burns, scolds and skin inflammations.

Sprite flails were made using nine bramble branches bound at the base by willow bark and were used to banish naughty or disruptive Nature spirits using the flail in the left hand (or the right hand if you were left handed). The five-petalled flowers were linked to the triple goddess as was the fruit with its three stages of colour: green, turning to red and then to black, being symbolic of the three aspects of the goddess — maiden, mother and Crone. The bramble was regarded as a fairy plant and picking the fruit after Samhain was considered back luck as it then belonged to the fairy folk although there are some who believed that eating a single fruit after this time would facilitate fairy contact; lying and meditating beneath a bramble thicket would do the same.

Bramble is linked to the goddess of joy, exhilaration and wrath, the temptress of the poet and bringer of intoxication. Her gift is double-edged and can bring inspiration or madness. Her teaching is deep and profound and poets and shamans drank bramble wine to inspire visions. But at that time the alcohol content of the wine was very high and there was a fine line between inspiration and intoxication. The related bird, the titmouse, is the king of the thicket and has mastered the ability to eat the fruit whilst not being caught by the thorns. If you are ever picking blackberries, it is always worth making an offering to honour the titmouse and ask for its help.

Gort

Letter: G
Tree: Gort — Ivy
Bird: Geis — Mute swan
Colour: Gorm — Blue
Original meaning: Scarcity; inadequate harvest
Numerological value: 6

The ivy has long been associated with taverns and intoxicating drinks as the Celts made ivy wine as a shamanic drink to inspire visions and prophetic dreams. Its leaves contain an active substance called hederin and were chewed to facilitate altered states of consciousness (note: today ivy is considered a poison and should not be ingested). The word **gort** is also thought to mean vineyard or garden and its original meaning of inadequate harvest may relate to the fact that ivy strangles trees and depletes their harvest of fruits. Perhaps this warned against allowing the energy of this plant to take over planting areas.

Ivy has strong associations with the feminine, and its five-lobed leaves are representative of the five aspects of woman. Its spiral growth pattern is symbolic of the spiral of life and its ever-green quality is highly prized in winter as a symbol of life in death. Druids would often decorate their shrines with ivy to attract Nature's spirits, especially at midwinter. The plant begins life as a weak and pliable shoot but after many years of growth forms very hard, woody stems that can support the plant to great heights. This makes it symbolic of transforming weakness to strength, and the fact that it cannot survive without its roots being firmly bedded in the earth teaches the need to be grounded in order to attain spiritual heights.

Medicinally, ivy leaves were infused and the tea drunk as an antidote to poison and an external salve was used to treat tired muscles. The mute swan, like ivy, is sacred to the goddess and symbolic of communication between different worlds being a bird of land, air and water. It is also symbolic of unconditional love, innocence and purity. The swan has a further link to ivy because it is a bird that is at home in a cold climate, provided there is food available, and so is often linked like ivy to winter.

Ngetal

Letter: Ng
Tree: Ngetal — Reed
Bird: Ngeigh — Goose
Colour: Nglas — Green
Original meaning: Preservation; the written word
Numerological value: 5

The reed was used by the Celts to make paper and pens, hence its association with the written word and the preservation of know-ledge. It was also used in thatching, floor covering and basket-making and musical reed pipes were used to call fairy spirits and give the player the ability to see into and travel within the fairy realm. The Mediterranean Celts used the *canna* reed to make arrow shafts that were exceedingly strong, yet hollow, making them per-fect carriers of poison and the Irish sun god, Lugh, was said to assert his authority and scatter his enemies by firing reed arrows.

Because it grows in and above water and its image is reflected in water, the reed is symbolic of interaction and integration between the two worlds. The solid reed represents the physical world and its reflection represents the elusive land of fairy. It is also associated with the dark portion of the year, the time of reflection and dreams. The correlation between the goose and the reed is easy to see. The goose takes refuge in the reed bed, flies in a V-formation like an arrowhead and its feathers, like reeds, were favoured as writing implements, all of which create further links with the symbolism of the written word.

Straif

Letter: St
Tree: Straif — Blackthorn
Bird: Stmolach — Thrush
Colour: Sorcha — Bright
Original meaning: Spiritual authority
Numerological value: 1

The blackthorn, or sloe, is a tree that grows both strong and dense, making it much favoured by the Celts for staffs, walking sticks, cudgels, clubs and shillelaghs. It has a strong masculine energy and grows into thick, thorny impenetrable barriers and so was often used in hedges and boundaries with its sister, the hawthorn. It is one of the earliest trees to flower and the arrival in Britain of the cold north-easterly winds in early spring often coincides with the flowering of the blackthorn; this is traditionally known as blackthorn winter. These potentially destructive winds were important for blowing away the old energies of winter to make way for the new growth of spring and thus the blackthorn was linked to the winds of change.

A wand made from blackthorn wood was considered very magical and was said to enable its owner to shapeshift from human form into animal form and back again. It was also used to return negative energy back to its source and for banishing dark spirits. Its long association with spiritual authority made it greatly favoured for staffs by Druids and shamans alike and its flowers were used medicinally to make a gargle for sore throats. The sloe berry produces a pigment dark enough to be used as permanent ink and any ogham written using this ink was considered especially powerful. The association with the thrush may be due to the fact that they were said to use blackthorn spines to impale snails on to extract them from their shells and the ancient collective noun for thrushes, a mutation, is another link to the power of change.

Ruis

Letter: R
Tree: Ruis — Elder
Bird: Rochat — Rook
Colour: Ruadh — Blood red
Original meaning: Eternity; sacred to the Crone
Numerological value: 22

The elder is a veritable medicine chest with its bark, leaves, flowers and berries being used to treat a wide range of ailments including bruises, wounds, chilblains, colds, respiratory problems and fevers. Its flowers and berries were used by the Celts to make wine that was said to aid fairy contact and elder whistles and flutes were said to call the fairies to dance. The Druids regarded any berries left on the tree in December as the last gift of the earth goddess before she retired to her winter rest; they collected them to make into a wine which was drunk to aid clairvoyance.

The elder has been linked to winter and death since before the Celts. Funerary flints have been found in megalithic long barrows in the shape of elder leaves and in some barrows a portal shaped like an elder leaf has been carved out between two slabs of stone. It is also often found growing on or around ancient graves. It had a reputation amongst the Celts as a tree of protection and was used to ward off negative energies and lightning. In Ireland it was used to make the shaft of the birch broom in favour of the more traditionally used ash and had strong links to the powers of magic and sorcery.

The elder's associated bird, the rook, was highly regarded as a bird of prophecy, and its collective noun, a parliament, originates from the Celtic belief that these birds sat and debated with one another.

Ailm

Letter: A
Tree: Ailm — Elm
Bird: Aidhircleog — Lapwing
Colour: Alad — Piebald
Original meaning: Rising above adversity; healing; foresight
Numerological value: 8

Until recently the elm was one of the commonest and tallest trees in the English forest. In a hundred years of growth it could reach heights in excess of 150 feet (45 metres) and live for over 400 years. Sadly, in the early part of the twentieth century, Dutch elm disease arrived in Britain and all the mature trees were killed. Nowadays elms only grow for about thirty years before the disease kills them and so this once majestic and magnificent tree has now been largely reduced to a hedgerow plant. Its original association with rising above adversity is on account of its great height and its longevity gave it an understanding of the patterns of the past; the Celts believed this enabled it to see the unfolding patterns of the future, hence its association with foresight. It was also said that picking an elm leaf and then placing it under your pillow before retiring would inspire prophetic dreams. The elm's Celtic association with the lapwing derived from the bird's reputation as a bird of divination and prophecy.

As a source of healing the elm had many uses. The leaves were applied to septic wounds as a poultice and chewing elm bark was a cure for toothache. The inner bark was used to treat skin conditions and a resinous substance called ulmin that exudes from the bark during the summer was a well-known treatment for ringworm. The elm had many practical uses too with its wood being prized for making tool handles, bridges, piles and boats.

Onn

Letter: O
Tree: Onn — Gorse
Bird: Odoroscrach — Cormorant
Colour: Odhar — Dun
Original meaning: Fertility
Numerological value: 7

Gorse is one of the few plants that can flower all year round, especially if the winter is mild, giving it its original meaning of fertility. It is certainly one of the first plants to flower and provides an important early food for bees. In the autumn gorse was burnt so that the thorns were destroyed; the new green shoots that sprang up after burning provided a valuable food for livestock whilst the ash enriched the soil. It will grow on even the poorest of soils, another connection with fertility, and was an excellent fire starter, burning fiercely even when green and with such intense heat as to set alight even the poorest of woods.

The Celts regarded gorse as the embodiment of both the masculine and feminine. The yellow flowers represented the young sun god whilst the green shoots represented the goddess who gave him life. The gorse is a favourite shelter for the hare, an animal that is sacred to the goddess. Like all thorny plants, gorse was also linked to psychic protection and it was thought that deep within gorse thickets were doorways to the Celtic Underworld. This may explain its link with the cormorant which in Celtic myth was an aquatic guide to the Underworld that was also accessed via the sea, lakes, rivers, springs and wells.

Ur

Letter: U
Tree: Ur — Heather
Bird: Uiseog — Skylark
Colour: Usgdha — Resinous
Original meaning: Luck; freshness
Numerological value: 3

Heather was a valuable resource from which brooms, ropes, insulation and thatching were made. It yields two excellent dyes, one green and one yellow, and also produces a mordant, which is a substance that allows cloth to accept the dye colour. It was much favoured as a bedding material equal in comfort to down and sleeping upon heather was believed to restore strength and refresh the spirit. Medicinally, heather had many uses, for example, as a general tonic, a specific tonic for heart and nerves and as a balm to relieve the discomfort of rheumatism.

The pre-Celtic Picts brewed ale from heather that required no sugar because of the richness of its nectar and was said to cleanse the blood. Heather's rich nectar is much favoured by bees and heather honey was highly prized amongst the Celts for its healing properties. The Celts regarded bees as spirit messengers who could travel the path of sunlight to the spirit world and return with wisdom that could be gained through eating honey.

The skylark is the only bird that habitually sings during all its flight. It sings whilst ascending almost vertically, whilst hovering in the air so high that it is almost out of sight and again whilst descending almost vertically. The Celts believed that this bird sang to bring joy both to gods and men. Hearing its song was a sign of good luck.

Eadha

Letter: E
Tree: Eadha — Aspen
Bird: Ela — Whistling swan
Colour: Erc — Red
Original meaning: Preventing death
Numerological value: 1

Aspen, or white poplar, was the most favoured wood for making shields in Celtic times and was said to protect one from death and disease. The Irish used an aspen rod called a **Fe** marked with ogham script to measure the dead for their coffins and graves. The aspen had strong associations with the Underworld and no one would touch a Fe except its owner for fear of being lured to the Underworld. Incidentally, today aspen is still used to make wooden rulers. Other uses for aspen included splints for holding broken bones in place, wagon bottoms and flooring. Medicinally, aspen is similar to willow in its therapeutic uses and was regarded as being effective in the treatment of fevers, pain, sore throats, coughs and skin ailments.

One of the unique characteristics of the aspen is that its leaves tremble in even the slightest breeze and Celtic bards and shamans would often divine by listening to the sounds made by the wind rustling its leaves. It was also a tree associated with the white goddess of death, and winter, the season when access to the Underworld was considered easiest. The whistling swan is unique to the swan family because its flight is silent and this gave it the reputation amongst the Celts as a bird that could retrieve lost souls that had been lured to the Underworld.

Iubhar

Letter: I
Tree: Iubhar — Yew
Bird: Illiat — Eaglet
Colour: Irfinf — White
Original meaning: The last day of the year; rebirth
Numerological value: 5

Throughout Europe the yew has always been associated with death, rebirth and immortality. It is the longest living of the native British trees and although after many centuries the central trunk becomes soft and decayed, a new tree grows within that becomes indistinguishable from its parent. Yews found growing in church-yards are often said to have been planted to ward off cattle as yew is poisonous to most animals, but this is not really true. Yews found growing in churchyards are more often a sign that the site was once sacred to the Celts. Many yews growing in churchyards are older than the Christianity of the area and this is because churches were built on old Celtic sacred sights and burial grounds in an attempt to destroy the ancient ceremonial practices of the Celts.

The Celts considered yew wood as the best wood for making bows and dagger hilts because of its durability and ease of carving. It is said that a yew fence post will outlast an iron one and its reputation for durability gave it the name 'the yew of resilience'. Oghams were often carved on yew rods for use in divination and it was considered one of the wisest and most magical trees of the forest. The berry of the yew, once distilled becomes one of the most active and potent vegetable poisons known to man. A small dose will lead to almost instant death. The Irish mixed it with hellebore and a plant called devil's bit to poison their weapons with.

In hot weather the yew gives off a vapour which shamans inhaled to promote visions, though sleeping under a yew tree in summer was said to induce a sleep so deep that the person becomes unrousable. The Irish called the yew the coffin of the vine because they used its wood to make wine barrels, perhaps to increase the visionary properties of the wine. Although it is associated with the goddess of death, with winter and the Underworld, because it is evergreen, the yew was linked to rebirth and the young eagle, the eaglet, associated with rebirth into spiritual wisdom.

The thirteen tree months

As well as using trees as the basis for a magical alphabet, the Celts also used thirteen of the ogham trees in a lunar calendar. This calendar provides an excellent form in which to discover more about the energies and teachings of trees. You can work with each tree for twenty-eight days researching its mythology, meditating with it and so on. It is not until you gain a personal relationship with each tree that its true wisdom can be accessed. The tree calendar gives guidance as to which trees to work with at which time of year to best understand their teachings.

It is interesting to note the positions of each tree because the allocation of each tree was based on the Celts' deep understanding of the energy and nature of trees. The hawthorn month coincides with the tree's flowering and the hazel month with its production of nuts. The oak month encompasses midsummer and this is followed by the holly month (remember the Holly King is reborn at midsummer). The bramble month coincides with its production of fruit, as does the ivy month. Some of the reasons why the Celts allocated other trees to certain months are less obvious but become more apparent as you work with and honour each tree.

Ogham name	Tree month	Dates
Beth	Birchmoon	24 December–20 January
Luis	Rowanmoon	21 January–17 February
Nion	Ashmoon	18 February–17 March
Fearn	Aldermoon	18 March–14 April
Saille	Willowmoon	15 April–12 May
Huath	Hawthornmoon	13 May–9 June
Duir	Oakmoon	10 June–7 July
Tinne	Hollymoon	8 July–4 August
Coll	Hazelmoon	5 August–1 September
Muin	Bramblemoon	2 September–29 September
Gort	Ivymoon	30 September–27 October
Ngetal	Reedmoon	28 October–24 November
Ruis	Eldermoon	25 November–22 December
Unnamed day 23 December		

Making an ogham set

Crafting your own set of ogham is an excellent way to get to know the Celtic trees and, as we shall see, you can also use your set to help guide you on your unfolding path. You can make the pieces out of wood, stone or clay and mark them by burning, painting or carving an ogham letter on each piece. The first ogham was written on birch and if you choose to use this wood, cutting one inch (2 to 3 cm) lengths of twig and marking them with each letter makes a very attractive set. Yew is another excellent wood to use. I made my first ogham set with a yew branch about two inches (5 cm) wide cut into half-inch (1 to 2 cm) circles and burnt using a pyrography set.

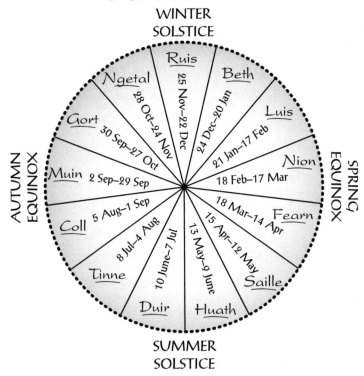

The thirteen tree months

If you go out into a forest or woodland to collect wood from a living tree for your ogham set or for any other purpose, it is always best to be guided by your intuition. Choose a tree that calls out to you, one you feel drawn to and make a physical connection with the tree. As you look at the tree, find a piece of it, for example, a branch, that you are attracted to whilst mentally or verbally explaining to the tree why you want to take a piece of it. Before you cut your piece of wood, it is always good to ask the tree's permission. Once you get used to listening to your intuition, the answer comes clearly into your mind but, if you are unclear as to the answer, look for a sign of confirmation from Nature around you. This may be an animal call, an unexpected breeze or a bird flying by that catches your eye. Go with your intuition and if everything feels fine, ask the tree to leave a little of its energy in the piece of wood you are going to cut to help and guide you. It is also nice to leave an offering of a little sea-salt (a traditional Celtic offering), tobacco, a piece of ribbon or your own hair as an exchange of energy.

Stone is another excellent medium to use for making an ogham set. You can collect pebbles or flat pieces of stone from a river-bed or beach and paint the ogham letters on them or even carve them if you feel more ambitious. I have seen metal ogham pendants in shops and they do look attractive so if you already work in metal, or feel drawn to take a craft course in metalwork, you might like to make a metal set. Whichever you choose, as you create your set, you should try to fill it with good thoughts and prayers. You may also wish to make or buy a special bag to house your set and personalise it with some simple embroidery. You do not have to be a great sewer or craftsperson to do this; you just need patience and a pure intent.

One of the best ways to personalise your set is to perform a simple ceremony to welcome it into your life and imbue it with positive energy. What I do is to first wash the set in a stream or cleanse it by passing it through the smoke of burning herbs or incense. This cleans the set of any negative energy and prepares it for consecration. Then I light a candle and say a few simple words of thanks for the set coming into my life and I usually make a personal commitment to only use the set for positive and good and to always treat it with love and respect. If you want to do a more elaborate ceremony, you can cleanse and empower your set by leaving it overnight under the light of the Full Moon. You can then wrap the set in a cloth with herbs in it, tie it with a ribbon and bury it in the ground. Then light a sacred fire over it and leave it buried until the next New Moon. This empowers the set with the energies of the four elements: Earth (the burial), Fire (the sacred fire), Air (the smoke) and Water (steam, dew and the earth's underground moisture). If there is a frost, snow or a thunderstorm whilst the set is buried, this is a blessing from creation and will make your set even more special. You may like to use this ceremony or create one of your own, but whatever you do, it should be done with a good and pure intent. Once you have made and blessed your set, it is unwise to lend it to anyone or let people play with it. This does not mean you become possessive, but the more you work with your set, the more accustomed it will become to your energy and you to it. If other energies come into long-term contact with it, your set will not work as well for you.

You can now begin to use your set as a teacher and guide in your spiritual life. The simplest place to start is by drawing out a single ogham each morning to act as your guide for the day. When you have drawn your ogham, meditate with it for a few minutes taking note of any thoughts or images that come to mind. Then look up the symbolism for the tree to give you an idea of what it has to teach you that day. If you can, go out and find the actual tree you have drawn and spend some time just being with its energy and getting to know it better. This will help you to better understand its wisdom and teaching.

As you become more familiar with your set, you can use it more extensively. For instance, if you have a problem or decision to make, you can draw three ogham to help put things into perspective. The first ogham comments on the past, the second shows you what you need to learn in the present and the third one shows you a possible future once you have learnt all you need to from the situation. For instance, if you drew duir (oak), saille (willow) and nion (ash), the interpretation might be that you have been over rigid and need more flexibility in your life that will give you the opportunity to integrate your spiritual, emotional and physical energies. Oak warns against rigidity, willow teaches flexibility and the ash represents the three worlds that in humans mean spirit, mind and body.

The more you work with trees, the more you will understand about their nature and in doing so will understand more about your own nature. Whether you live in a city or the country, there are always trees that you can meet and interact with. Each tree is unique and special, but every once in a while you will encounter a tree that is truly remarkable and rich in character. Its beauty of form and energy will leave you speechless and you will have experienced first hand the magic of this wonderful and diverse realm of creation. Trees can become familiar friends and given time they will communicate with you and teach you many lessons.

Six

CELTIC ANIMAL MEDICINE

The Celts regarded all animals as sacred, each one having its own unique energy or spirit that could be communicated with. The Celtic shamans were skilled in the art of shapeshifting. This allowed them to assume any form and to experience what it was like to be an animal, a stone or a plant. Celtic literature abounds with stories of shapeshifting and the most famous is the story of Cerridwen and Gwion. Cerridwen was a sorceress who gave birth to a very ugly son who she called Avagdu, which means 'Utter Darkness'. Realising that his ugliness could make him a social outcast, she resolved to create a spell to imbue him with great knowledge and wisdom. This, she thought, would make him popular despite his ugliness. The spell she wove involved cooking a potion for a year and a day in a cauldron heated by a log fire. She employed a young man named Gwion Bach ('Gwion the Little'), son of Gwreang of Llanfair, to stir the potion and a blind man called Morda to stoke the fire. When the potion was nearly ready, three drops of it spat out of the cauldron and on to Gwion's hand. To relieve the burn, he sucked his fingers and thus took the energy of the potion into his body. He was immediately bestowed with all the knowledge and wisdom that was meant for Cerridwen's son. The potion, now devoid of its magic turned to a bitter poison that melted the cauldron and ran into a nearby stream. A man called Gwyddno Garanhir took his horses to drink at the stream and they all died. After that the stream was known as the Poison of the Horses of Gwyddno.

Realising the sorceress would be angry with him, Gwion fled but Cerridwen soon discovered what had occurred and, intent on revenge, pursued him. Gwion, with his now heightened senses felt her nearing presence and changed himself into a hare, where-upon Cerridwen changed into a greyhound. Leaping into a river, Gwion changed himself into a fish but Cerridwen leapt after him, transforming herself into an otter as she entered the water. Gwion then transformed himself into a bird; Cerridwen changed herself into a hawk. Finally Gwion turned himself into a grain of sand but Cerridwen then changed into a hen and ate him. Nine months later she gave birth to him as an infant and would have killed him were it not for his outstanding beauty. Instead, she wrapped him in a leather bag and threw him into the sea to the mercy of God.

Now, Gwyddno, of the poisoned horses, owned a salmon weir and was there one day with his son Elphin. Elphin was a very needy lad who had had little luck in his life so far and this day was playing as usual by the weir when he suddenly spied a leather bag floating towards him. He plucked it from the water and ran with it to his father who opened it. Inside was an infant of such beauty that Gwyddno exclaimed, 'Behold Taliesin', which means 'Radiant Brow', to which Elphin said, 'Taliesin be he called.' They brought the child home and raised it as their own. The child grew to be Taliesin, the greatest Celtic bard; and the first poems he made were praising his finder, Elphin and promising him good fortune. And Taliesin's prophecy was fulfilled for Elphin grew in both stature and riches, finding favour in love and with the king.

This story is typical in structure of many of the Celtic tales. There are changes in reality or in the perception of reality, there is a conflict, there are animals and there is a secondary group of characters whose lives are interwoven with that of the hero. Gwyddno first loses his horses but later gains a son (Taliesin) who changes his life and the life of his son, Elphin. Such stories are multi-layered and rich in symbolism with every detail being sig-nificant. It is no coincidence that when the humble Gwion is reborn as the wise and learned Taliesin, he is found in a salmon weir because the Celts regarded the salmon as the oldest and wis-est of all creatures. To the Celts everything had significance and meaning and especially noted were encounters with animals.

In the Celtic multi-dimensional world there were many different animals of all shapes and sizes, each with their own characteristics and medicine to teach. The Celts encountered animals, not only in the physical realm, but also in the Otherworld. These magical creatures were often distinguishable by an unearthly white colour and equally unearthly red teeth and/or ears. An encounter with such an animal, be it a stag, boar or hound, was an indication to a shaman that he had entered another reality. In the Celtic world it was normal to slip from one reality into another. The natural world was full of magical places where the veil between this world and the land of fairy was very thin, where one could step through without even realising.

In the Welsh *Mabinogion*, a collection of Celtic tales, there is a story about Pwyll, Lord of Dyfed. Pwyll was out one day hunting with his men and hounds when a strange mist came down. Pwyll became separated from his men and lost contact with them without noticing it while his hounds were on the scent of a stag. He heard the sound of a hunting horn and followed its sound with his dogs. Soon they came upon another group of hounds that had brought down a deer. These dogs had white coats with red ears and this should have told Pwyll that he had crossed through the veil into the Otherworld. But he did not realise and allowed his own hounds to chase away the fairy dogs with a view to keeping the kill for himself.

Soon the owner of the fairy dogs arrived. It was Arawn, King of the Underworld, who was much angered that his hounds had been chased from their kill. To appease Arawn, Pwyll was forced to change places with him for a year and at the end of the year kill Hafgan, Arawn's enemy. This he does and thereafter he and Arawn become firm friends and enjoy many friendly encounters.

Again we have the themes of conflict, animals and different realities. To have to live in the Underworld for a year might seem a high price to pay for taking a deer, but one has to remember that in the Celtic Otherworld, the concepts of space and time are not the same as in the physical world. A year in the Otherworld can be equivalent to a day in this world, but the opposite can also be true. The Irish hero Oisin travels to the land of fairy and stays there but a few years before returning to his homeland only to find that 300 years have passed.

It is quite clear from reading the Celtic myths that many encounters with animals were of a shamanic nature. Shamans could spiritually travel to other realms and learn about the universe without the constraints of the physical world. Animals could be conversed with through telepathy and ancient or magical creatures actually spoke the language of humans, especially birds. This allowed Celtic shamans/heroes to be forewarned of dangers and to learn secret healing knowledge. All animals had their symbolism and lessons to teach and many were allies on shamanic journeys to the Otherworld.

Each Celtic tribe had its own totem animal and it was forbidden for any member of the tribe to eat the flesh of that animal. Shamans too had their personal animal helpers or guides and it was taboo to eat, hunt or in any way harm these animals. This taboo was called a **geis** and keeping to it was regarded as a matter of life or death. There are several stories of heroes breaking their geis and dying as a result. Before I knew of this practice, I had found myself naturally doing it. One of the first creatures to appear to me in a vision was a stag. It is an animal that has taught me a great deal and since this first encounter I have lost the urge to eat venison, meat that prior to this time had been a favourite of mine. This is not so strange because once you make a personal connection with an animal a spiritual relationship builds up and the animal becomes a friend. You wouldn't consider eating your pet dog or cat and I feel the same way about my personal power animals.

I find that as I journey through life, different animals come to me to teach me. They usually first appear in a dream or vision, sometimes talking, sometimes not. I then often find a physical confirmation that the animal wants to work with me. Shortly after my vision of a stag, I was given a set of antlers by a friend and deer regularly appeared to me on walks in the woods and whilst driving. A single sighting of a deer may be coincidence, but when they appear on a daily basis, one tends to take note. I was even led one day to a whole stag skeleton whilst on a walk in the woods. I was walking in woodland that I had visited on an almost weekly basis for the past four years. Suddenly a voice in my head told me to walk towards a particular yew tree and as I did so I came across the complete skeleton of a stag. It had obviously been lying there for several years as the skull had a good deal of lichen growing on it. The incredible thing is that I had walked past that very spot many times and never seen it. It must have been there all the time but was somehow hidden from my view. Also strange was the fact that the skeleton was complete. Usually foxes, dogs and other animals find the bones, but this skeleton was untouched. It was almost as if the stag had died and travelled to the Otherworld taking its bones with it and only returning them several years later.

This is how it is when you begin to work spiritually with animals. Artefacts such as bones, skulls, teeth, fur or feathers begin to manifest into your life with such regularity that it can no longer be coincidence. Recently I was walking in the woods with a friend, Laura, who was going to keep fire for a ceremony that evening. We were walking together when we both let out an exclamation of wonder as we each spotted a buzzard feather on the path in front of us. The amazing thing was that we each spotted different feathers, one on each side of the path and neither of us were aware of the other feather lying but a few feet away. The chances of finding two such feathers lying so close is remote and we took it as a sign that our ceremony would go well, which it did. The relationship and understanding between a shaman and fire-keeper during a ceremony is very important and it was as if the feathers gave Laura and me a connection that helped us work better together.

As you begin to work with animal energies, you begin to understand that they are more than simple creatures. They are teachers with many lessons to teach to those willing to learn. Each animal has its own characteristics and resources that we can learn and draw inspiration from. To the Celts every animal had a purpose and medicine to give. This medicine took the form of insights and understandings that changed perceptions and brought healing. Remember, all illness begins in the mind. So, if an encounter with an animal makes you change your thinking, it will have a beneficial effect on your health overall. Let us now look at some of the major Celtic animals, their symbolism and teachings.

Animals on the Wheel of Life

The feathered ones

To the Celts birds were creatures of great wisdom and teaching. They appear throughout the Celtic myths and many are possessed with supernatural powers. The Welsh goddess Rhiannon is portrayed with three magical birds whose songs could 'awaken the dead and lull the living to sleep'. Cliodna, another Celtic heroin also has three magical birds that heal the sick and wounded with their enchanted songs. Birds often symbolise the flight of the spirit to the Otherworld and most were regarded as being able to travel between worlds. Perhaps this is because they spend much of their time between the worlds of heaven and earth in flight.

The Celts wore feathers in their hair and on their clothing to attune them to the energy and teaching of a particular bird. Chieftains wore eagle feathers as a sign of authority whilst shamans wore cloaks of crow feathers to aid them in their travels to other realms. The Druids were skilled in the art of augury, which is divining through observation of the activities and songs of birds. They domesticated ravens as divinatory birds and, as we have already seen, linked the divinatory meaning of trees with specific birds. They particularly favoured the wren as a divinatory bird and the direction in which the bird appeared was given great meaning. Swans and eagles appeared as omens in Celtic myth and whether their appearance was good or bad depended on the day that they appeared. Many heroes had birds as their totem animals and were therefore not permitted to hunt or eat them. The Irish hero, Cuchulainn, chief of the Ultonians, had a geis against killing or eating swans because his mother Deichtire had the swan as her totem.

Birds appear in dreams and visions as well as the physical world. Often, if I dream about a particular bird, I will find a feather from that bird when I am out walking. This acts as a confirmation that the bird is trying to teach me something. The summer is the time of year when many birds moult and so it is more common to find feathers at this time, though I have found some beautiful feathers in the middle of winter. The trick to finding beautiful feathers is to not look for them. I have always found that if I have been consciously looking for feathers I find none, but when I have not even been thinking about them, feathers have found me. It is almost as if they jump out at you with their vibrant energy and grab your attention.

As you get to understand the energies of birds better, they become more willing to show themselves to you. Most times when I light a sacred fire, owls come near and call to me. During a ceremony at the last solar eclipse, a buzzard swooped low down over us in the middle of it and we have often had one or more circling high overhead as we have prepared for an evening ceremony. Another time I was driving along when I came across two magpies dead in the road. A car had obviously hit them, but the fact that they had been killed together was unusual so I honoured their lives by taking them home and making a shield out of their wings, tails and claws. After that I had many interesting encounters with magpies, both in visions and in this world.

There are many birds that appear in Celtic myth and we can learn much from studying their symbolism and meaning.

The wren

The smallest of the British birds, the wren was highly regarded by the Druids as a bird of augury and indeed the Welsh word for wren 'drui-en', literally means 'Druid's bird'. The direction in which the wren appears, the frequency of its call, where it alighted and so on all had specific meanings, from foretelling the arrival of visitors to predicting death. Its title, the 'king of birds', originates from a Celtic myth describing the manner in which the birds decided who should be their king. The story tells that the birds decided whichever of them could fly highest would be crowned king. The eagle knew that he could fly the highest and confidently soared up to the heavens but as he reached his maximum height the wren, which had hidden on his back, flew that little bit higher and so was crowned king. Because of its sovereignty, hunting or killing it was forbidden, except during the midwinter feast. The wren was linked to the oak, the summer king, whose death at midwinter marked the death of the old year. I believe that the wren was originally merely captured at midwinter and suspect that the idea of killing it at midwinter may have originated from the church trying to stamp out Druidic practices.

In Welsh myth, Lleu Llaw Gyffes ('Bright One of the Skilful Hand') gets his name when his mother, Arianrhod, witnesses him hitting a wren on the leg with a stone, a near impossible feat given the diminutive size and rapid, erratic flight of the bird. Another Celtic hero, Cuchulainn also demonstrates the same skill although his son, Connla, is even more skilled, being able to catch a bird by stunning it only with his singing. As a prophetic bird, the wren is sacred to Taliesin and if one appears to you, you should always take note for it is trying to tell you something.

The eagle

The eagle was regarded as one of the oldest and wisest of all birds. The Welsh *Mabinogion* tells a story of how Lleu Llaw Gyffes was tricked by his unfaithful wife, Blodeuwedd, into revealing the manner in which he could be killed. Her lover, Gronw, is hiding nearby and when Lleu is showing his wife how he can be killed Gronw runs him through with a poisoned spear. Lleu immediately shapeshifts into an eagle and flies up into an oak tree, where he is later found by the magician Gwydion and restored to health. The symbolism in this story points clearly to the eagle as a solar bird. Lleu is the Welsh sun god and the oak is also linked to the power of the sun.

The eagle teaches objectivity and clear-sightedness and if one appears to you, either in a dream or real life, it is a sign to take a step back and look objectively at where you are in life.

The owl

The owl, being a creature of the night, is linked to the dark and hidden side of human nature. In the story of Lleu's attempted assassination, Blodeuwedd is punished for her treachery by being turned into an owl. By doing this, Lleu, the solar god who rules the daytime, makes certain that their paths will never again cross because the owl is a bird of the night. To many people the owl is a dark omen but to me it teaches the power of deception and discernment and how to learn from and master the darker side of our nature. It is generally regarded throughout Europe as a bird of great wisdom with the power to see clearly when others see only darkness and gloom.

The owl teaches discernment of truth both in yourself and those you meet.

The swan

Throughout Celtic legend Swans are linked with the Underworld and Samhain, the festival when the veil between this world and the Underworld is at its thinnest. Swans are often described as metamorphosed women linked together by gold and silver chains.

In one Celtic tale, Oenghus dreams of a beautiful girl called Caer Ibormeith ('Yew Berry') and discovers that she lives by a lake with 150 other young women. The tale tells how every alternate year at Samhain, she and her companions are transformed into swans. The swans are linked in pairs by silver chains except Caer who is described as the tallest and has a gold chain denoting her higher status. To woo her, Oenghus transforms himself into a swan and the two fly off together back to Oenghus's home where they lull everyone to sleep for three days and nights with their beautiful song. There are other stories that also tell of the enchanting song of the swan and it was often the totemic bird of bards, the Celtic shaman-poets and songsters.

The swan teaches clarity and purity of thought and comes to help one gain a stronger spiritual connection with creation.

The crane
This bird too is linked to women, but more often to the darker side of the feminine. It is usually linked with death and the Underworld as in the story of the Irish hero, Finn, who has an encounter with Cailleach an Teampuill ('The Hag of the Temple') and her four sons. The sons appear in the form of four death cranes who can only become human again if they are sprinkled with the blood of a magical bull. The cry of the crane too is linked to the Hag, the most powerful and dark aspect of the triple goddess. Manannan Mac Lir, the Irish sea god, had a magical bag made from the skin of a crane that was once a woman who was transformed into a crane on account of her jealous nature. All these images made the crane both feared and highly respected in Celtic tradition and in early Ireland eating crane flesh was strictly forbidden for fear that one might be really eating the flesh of the dark goddess.

The crane, with its death symbolism, teaches us how to let go of the past and embrace the ever-changing future.

The crow, the raven and the magpie
All these birds are linked with death, destruction and war and are sacred to the Crone, the alternative name for the Hag aspect of

the triple goddess. Indeed the word 'crone' is thought to originate
from either the Old Dutch word 'croonje' meaning carcass, or the
Old Northern French word 'carogne' meaning carrion. Their link
to death and war is most likely because these bird were often seen
feeding on corpses left on the battlefield.

Ravens were also seen as prophets, usually foretelling death,
as can be seen in the stories of the Irish war goddess, The
Morrigan. She is a threefold goddess who often appears as one or
three ravens and advises the Dagdha (one of the great kings of
the tribe of the Tuatha De Danann) as to the outcome of future
battles.

The crow, the raven and the magpie come to teach us to let
go of negative thoughts and to banish fear.

The woodpecker

The great spotted woodpecker carries three colours — red, white
and black — the colours of the triple goddess, and was a faithful
companion of Merlin, the most famous Celtic shaman/magician. It
was regarded as a bird of prophecy and longevity and its drumming was interpreted for divination. It was said that it strengthened
its beak by rubbing it on a sacred plant on midsummer's eve. In
some parts it was traditional to lay a red cloth beneath a woodpecker's nest on midsummer's day to catch the plant as it fell and
this was used as a charm to open locks.

The woodpecker teaches tenacity and determination and helps
one to clearly walk the spiritual path onwards and upwards.

The cockerel and the hen

In the Celtic tradition the cockerel did not welcome the rising of
the sun with its early morning call — instead, it chased away the
dark spirits of the night. It had strong links with masculine fertility
and was sacrificed to the goddess Brighid at her festival of Imbolc.
In some parts it was associated with the spirit of the corn and was
sacrificed at the end of the harvest season to ensure a fertile crop
the next year. As I have already explained, sacrifice in Celtic times
was a relatively rare occurrence, set aside for special occasions,

and it was only permitted to kill most sacred birds on one specific day of the year.

The hen too was linked to fertility as seen in the story of Cerridwen and Gwion. At the end of the harvest season, chickens were let loose into the fields to eat any discarded grain and free the land from potentially destructive insects, thus protecting the next crop from pests and ensuring its continued fertility.

The cockerel and the hen teach the power of new enlightenments and understandings.

The goose
This bird was strongly associated with warriors and its bones have regularly been found in Celtic warrior graves. It was traditionally sacrificed and eaten at the autumn equinox and was linked with protection of the home during the dark period of the year.

The goose teaches how to protect one's personal space from both physical and psychic negative influences and its feathers can be used to clear houses and ceremonial sites of negativity.

The blackbird
This wonderfully tuneful songbird was linked to the Celtic Otherworld and its singing at twilight was said to enable the listener to gain access to the land of fairy. The three magical birds of Rhiannon are often thought to have been blackbirds and so blackbirds are also strongly linked to healing.

The blackbird teaches how to find more balance and harmony in one's life.

The land-dwellers
The Celts were by and large nomadic hunter–gatherers and as such would have regularly encountered a wide variety of creatures. They were skilled trackers and hunters and would have known a great deal about the character and habits of every creature. Each animal had its own strengths and weaknesses and the Celtic shamans would often communicate with the spirit of a particular animal in order to gain wisdom, knowledge or that animal's

protection for the tribe. Before a hunt, there would be ceremony performed to communicate with the guardian spirit of the animal to be hunted to honour its life and teaching. Many animals had Otherworldly counterparts with magical qualities and higher spiritual teachings to impart. In the heat of the chase, it was not unusual for an animal to cross the veil between this world and the Otherworld or for a magical version of the hunted animal to appear in this world.

The boar and the sow

Wild boar roamed throughout the Celtic lands and were revered for their strength and ferocity. More than any other creature the wild boar symbolised warfare and aggression as seen in stone carvings of the British war god Cocidius who was often depicted carrying a spear with a boar by his side. Hunting boar was part of the Celtic rites of passage for young warriors as these creatures were notoriously hard to kill and in Celtic legend there are many stories of epic hunts. Otherworldly boars appear throughout Celtic myth in a variety of shapes and sizes. The *Mabinogion* tells of an encounter with a giant white boar by Pryderi and Manawydan and later in the same tale a giant named Ysbaddaden demands of Culhwch the tusk from another giant boar to use as a razor for shaving.

Of particular importance were the bristles of the boar. They are symbols of strength and power and were highly prized as magical weapons. Some bristles are poisonous, as in the story of Fion who is killed by stepping on a boar's bristle after breaking his geis against hunting boars. Others are made of silver or gold. There is even a story about two pig herders who are named Friuch and Rucht after the bristle and grunt of the boar respectively. Sows too were highly revered and sacred to the goddess Cerridwen who is often called 'The White Sow'.

Throughout Celtic myth the boar symbolises the power of male potency and the sun, whilst the sow symbolises female sensuality and the moon. Both animals teach strength and endurance, making them powerful allies on the spiritual path.

The bull and the cow

To the Celts the bull epitomised strength, potency and fertility and had a unique connection with kingship. In one Druid ritual called **tardh feis** ('bull feast'), the Druid/shaman would eat the flesh of a freshly slaughtered white bull and then wrap him/herself in its hide. He or she would then lie down and go to sleep whilst four Druids chanted around them. This induced a prophetic dream foretelling who should reign as the rightful king. The midwinter ceremonies often involved the sacrifice of a white bull and this coincided with the cutting of the sacred mistletoe on the morning of the sixth day of the New Moon. The famous Gundestrup Cauldron has two scenes involving bulls, one showing a slaughtered bull whilst the other shows a giant bull being attacked by three sword-wielding warriors.

One of the most famous Celtic legends is entitled *Táin Bó Cualnge* or *The Cattle Raid of Cooley*, and tells of an epic struggle for possession of the Brown Bull of Quelgny between Ailell and Maev, the king and queen of Connacht and Dara of Ulster who owned the Bull. Maev had her own bull named Finnbenach that was red in colour with a white front and horns, but it had attached itself to Ailell's herd and so to out-do her husband she sought a better bull. The Brown Bull of Quelgny was the mightiest beast in all Ireland having a back broad enough for fifty children to play on and when angered was said to stamp its keeper thirty feet into the ground. It must have been a magnificent animal because the writer likens it to a sea wave, to a bear, a dragon and a lion to convey its strength and might. Legend tells that Finnbenach and the Brown Bull of Quelgny are arch rivals and magical in origin with both being skilled in the art of shapeshifting. For one year they fought as ravens, for two years as water monsters, then as humans and finally as eels before both were eaten by cows and reborn as bulls. 'Finn' means 'fair' and so the saga is almost certainly a representation of the forces of light and dark in their constant flux and motion with neither ever gaining ascendance.

The cow is sacred to the goddess Brighid, who according to legend was born in the house of a Druid and fed on milk from a

sacred, Otherworldly cow with red ears. Fairy cattle appear frequently in Celtic myth with a variety of magical attributes and the
number three is often associated with them. Some are said to yield
three times more milk than a normal cow and three of the **crodh
mara** ('sea cattle') came ashore at Baile Cronon, one red, one
white and one black representing the three aspects of the goddess.
The cow is linked to a variety of gods and goddesses throughout
Celtic myth, including the goddess Boann (also called 'She of the
White Cows'), the Irish father god Dagdha (who owned an
enchanted black-maned heifer called 'Ocean') and the sea god
Manannan Mac Lir (guardian of the crodh mara). At the festival of
Beltane, cattle were driven between 'needfires' as a means of
purification before being moved to summer pastures and to aid
the fertility of the herd.

The cow and bull teach the need for balance between all
things and of the nature of the interaction between the light and
dark energies of the universe.

The horse

The Celts were master horsemen and used horses for hunting
and in battle. The ancient art of 'horse whispering' is said to have
originated in the pre-Celtic Pictish tribes of north-east Scotland
and were passed on to the Celts when they arrived in those lands.
Horses were linked to both gods and goddesses and were symbolic of strength, swiftness, fertility, motherhood and death.

The most famous Celtic horse story comes from the *Mabinogion*
and features the horse goddess Rhiannon. The story begins by
telling of a sacred mound at Narberth that was said to make one
of two things happen to anyone that sat on it: either he or she
received wounds and blows or they saw a wonder. Now it happened that one day Pwyll, Lord of Dyfed, was out with his men
when he came across the mound and decided to sit on it himself.
He received neither wounds nor blows but had not been sitting for
long when there appeared riding past 'a lady on a pure white horse
of large size, with a garment of shining gold around her'. Pwyll was
struck by her beauty and sent one of his men on foot to run to

her and enquire her name and place of origin. But, although the lady appeared to be riding at a slow pace, no matter how hard the man tried, he could not catch her and she soon rode out of sight.

The next day Pwyll returned to the mound at the same time and the lady on the white horse appeared again, riding slowly past. This time Pwyll sent a horseman after her and at first the horseman rode at a pace that seemed to be slightly greater than that of the lady but he came no nearer to her. He urged his horse into a gallop but still could gain no ground on her and soon she was once again out of sight. The next day Pwyll returned with his swiftest horse and determined to pursue the lady himself if she appeared. Sure enough, at the same time the lady came riding by and this time Pwyll mounted his horse and followed her. At first he rode at a gentle pace for the lady seemed to be riding at little more than a trot, but he gained no ground on her. He then rode his horse at its topmost speed but, if anything, he seemed to be getting further from her. In desperation he called out for her to stop. She replied, 'I will stop gladly and it would have been better for your horse if you had asked earlier.' She then went on to tell him that her name was Rhiannon, daughter of Heveydd the Ancient, and that she was to be married to a man she did not love and that would much rather marry Pwyll. This delighted Pwyll and he immediately asked for her hand in marriage to which she consented. The couple arranged to meet in a year and a day to be wed at Heveydd's palace and a great feast was prepared to welcome the Pwyll prior to the marriage.

On the appointed day Pwyll and a hundred of his most faithful followers journeyed to Heveydd's palace and received a rapturous welcome. Pwyll sat between Heveydd and Rhiannon and as they were feasting a beggar came into the hall and asked a boon of Pwyll. 'This is a joyous day for me,' said Pwyll, 'And whatever you ask, if it be in my power to give you, I will.' At this, the beggar threw off his disguise and said, 'I ask for the hand of Rhiannon in marriage.' Pwyll was dumbfounded and as a man of his word had to consent. The beggar was none other than Gwawl, the son of Clıd, the very man that Rhiannon had previously been betrothed to.

A further pre-wedding feast was arranged for a year and a day and, when the time came, it was Pwyll this time that entered the court disguised as a beggar, and carrying a small leather bag. Pwyll asked of Gwawl a boon, to which he asked, 'What do you seek?' 'Only enough meat to fill this bag,' said Pwyll and Gwawl instructed his men to fill the bag. But the more meat the men put in the bag, the more room appeared to be in it. The bag was a magical bag given to Pwyll by Rhiannon with instructions on how to use it. When Gwawl enquired as to the problem, Pwyll replied, 'The bag will only be filled if the food is trodden down by both feet of a noble man with land and riches.' Gwawl consented to tread down the food but no sooner had he put both feet into the bag than Pwyll pulled the bag over his head and with his men, who had been hiding, began to beat the bag. Fortunately for Gwawl, Heveydd intervened and Pwyll agreed to free Gwawl on the condition that he gave up all designs on marriage to Rhiannon and sought no revenge for having been tricked. Gwawl consented and Rhiannon and Pwyll were finally married.

There are many other stories involving horses and many different deities, both male and female, are linked to them. However, the main Celtic horse deities seem to be female and include Rhiannon, Epona (the Gaulish horse goddess), Medb (the Irish warrior goddess) and Cailleach (the Scottish crone goddess of healing wells who is described as having a blue-black face with a single eye in the centre of her forehead).

Horses usually represent positive omens and often teach how to embrace change and spiritual transformations.

The stag and the hind

The Celts linked the stag with wild Nature and Cernunnos, the lord of the animals, and the hind with the goddess Flidhais, who rules over all wild beasts and whose deer provide her with milk to drink. The story of Pwyll's encounter with Arawn shows that deer were prized both in this world and the Otherworld and indeed in Scotland they are referred to as 'fairy cattle'. The stag was a powerful totem of the shaman and in one story Merlin kills with a pair of stag's antlers the man who is to marry Guendoloena, who was once his own wife. White stags were regarded as particularly sacred and were linked to healing and hope and the Stag of Redynvre in the *Mabinogion* is one of the oldest and wisest of all creatures.

The hind, the female counterpart to the stag, is linked to shapeshifting and there are many stories of men being lured into the Otherworld by an enchanted hind that disappears and is replaced by a beautiful maiden.

The stag and the hind both teach how to tune into the subtler vibrations of creation and inspire dreams and visions.

The hound

Dogs were highly valued as companions and protectors and as well as being linked to hunting they were also associated with healing. They are often portrayed in Celtic myth as the companions of kings and warriors and were sacred to the goddess Nehalennia and the god Nodens. Being noted for their ability to see the unseen, dogs were regarded as protectors from supernatural beings as well as from animal and human enemies. Otherworldly dogs come in all shapes and sizes from the Scottish **dobhar-chu** ('water dogs') to the **madadh dubh** ('black dogs') who were said to haunt castles and sacred sites. The most famous Otherworldly dogs are the hounds of the wild hunt that are white with red ears and red teeth. The pack is led by Arawn, Lord of Annwn (the Underworld), and is said to conduct the dead to the Underworld. Some tales have Herne the Hunter as the leader of the pack who, according to local legend, still lives in the forests of Windsor Great Park, England, whilst others tell of the hunt being seen riding across the skies of Somerset and Devon on the night of the Full Moon.

The hound teaches keenness of sense and awareness of the unseen forces that pervade the earth.

The wolf, the bear and the badger

These three animals were all highly prized for their skins, which have frequently been found in the graves of Celtic chieftains. They appear relatively rarely in Celtic mythology but there are enough references to gain an understanding of how the Celts viewed these animals. Wolves symbolised motherhood and there are several tales of infants being reared and suckled by wolves. The Irish king, Cormac MacAirt, was reared by a she-wolf, as were the Celtic saints, St. Ailbe and St. Ciwa, the latter, not only being reared by a wolf, but also displaying a wolf claw on one of her hands.

The bear has been revered since prehistory with archaeological evidence dating back to Neanderthal times when bear skulls were used as altars. The Celtic name for bear is 'Artos' and variants of it are found in many of the names of heroes, including Andarta ('Strong Bear'), Arthur (from the Welsh 'Arth Vawr' meaning 'Great Bear') and Arthgen/Artigenous (Welsh/Irish meaning 'Son of the Bear').

The badger, a cousin of the bear, was traditionally regarded as a guide in the land of dreams. The ancient game of 'Badger in the Bag' is said to have originated from the incident related above where Pwyll and his men kicked Gwawl who had been tricked and captured in a magic bag and kicked around the floor of Heveydd's palace.

The wolf teaches feminine wisdom; the bear, strength; and the badger acts as a guide, not only in the dreamworld, but also in the unconscious mind.

The cat

The cat in Celtic times was a wild and extremely fierce animal that was either black or speckled in colour. Some people believe that this animal still survives and is behind the numerous stories of giant black cats such as 'The Beast of Bodmin' and 'The Exmoor Panther' seen on the moors and in remote regions of Britain. The Celts considered the cat a magical animal that, if approached with great respect and caution, would impart wisdom to those that sought it. It was usually linked to a goddess or sorceress, which may account for its later description as the witch's familiar.

It teaches resourcefulness and makes a valiant ally in all difficult undertakings.

The hare, the fox and the mouse

The hare was sacred to hunters and the moon goddess and was regarded as an oracular animal. The famous Celtic queen, Boudicca of the Iceni, kept a sacred hare and would release it prior to a battle. She would divine the outcome of the battle by studying the direction it took and the nature of its movements.

The famous Celtic bard Taliesin refers to the 'satirising fox' but beyond that there is little written about this mammal, although fox pelts have been found in several Celtic graves indicating it was keenly hunted for its fur.

The mouse appears several times in Celtic myth and most notably in the *Mabinogion* where Manawydan is about to kill one of many mice that have devastated his grain harvest when the creature reveals itself as the wife of the magician Llwyd. In return for his wife's life, Llwyd lifts an enchantment that has been placed upon the land causing widespread crop failure.

The hare teaches spontaneity, the fox new perspectives, especially with regard to problems and the mouse appreciation of the smaller blessings in life. The mouse also makes a fine ally if one is trying to communicate with the elemental energies of grains.

The water-dwellers

The Celts were keen sailors and fishermen and there is growing evidence to suggest that they crossed the Atlantic Ocean to America long before Christopher Columbus. They regarded water as another of the many veils between this world and the Otherworld, whether in the form of rivers, streams, pools or oceans, and all of the creatures that inhabited these places had strong Otherworld connections.

The salmon

The salmon was considered the oldest and wisest of all creatures. In Ireland it was forbidden for ordinary folk to catch or eat this fish for it was regarded as the food of kings. The Salmon of Llyn Llw was a gigantic fish on whose shoulders Culhwch and Gwrhyr travel in search of the divine child, Mabon. This was one of

thirty-nine tasks Culhwch has to carry out in order to prove his
love for Olwen, the daughter of a giant named Ysbaddaden. He
enlisted the help of Gwrhyr who had the gift of animal speech
and the two of them meet ever more ancient and wise animals.
First they meet the Blackbird of Cilgwri, who directs them to the
Stag of Rhedynfrc. He in turn sends them to the Owl of Cwn
Cawlwyd. The Owl sends them to the Eagle of Gwernabwy who
finally directs them to the Salmon of Llyn Llw who helps them find
the lost child.

In another story that has some similarities with the tale of
Cerridwen and Gwion, Fintan, an Irishman, was warned of a great
flood and transformed himself into a salmon and lived to a great
age. He lived in an enchanted well beneath the sea and around
this well grew the Nine Hazels of Wisdom, magical trees that pro-
duced both flowers and leaves in the same hour and whose nuts
imparted the secrets of great knowledge to any who ate them. The
nuts fell into the well and were eaten by Fintan and thus he
became the Salmon of Knowledge. A Druid named Finegas caught
Fintan and cooked him on a spit with a view to eating him and
thus gaining his knowledge and he employed his pupil, Finn
MacCumhail, to turn the spit. As Finn was minding the salmon, he
burnt his thumb on the fish and sucked it to relieve the pain.
Instantly he was imbued with the knowledge of all things. When
Finegas returned he noticed that Finn had changed and after
enquiring what had happened, told Finn to eat the fish himself,
adding that he had nothing more to teach him.

The salmon teaches us how to access inner wisdom to bring
emotional balance and calm.

The trout

In Celtic mythology the trout too is a fish of wisdom and has the
reputation of having strong links to the Otherworld. There are
stories of trout that, once captured, turn into beautiful fairy women
and others of trout that are only visible to those with second sight.
The Celts imitated the movements of the trout in a spring fertility
dance called 'Springing of the Trout' and the art of trout-tickling,

capturing a trout without the aid of hooks or nets, may well have originated with the Celts.

The trout teaches how to connect with spiritual wisdoms that can bring about new understandings and enlightenments.

The eel

Eels too were symbolic of wisdom, but also of warfare and protection. In the story of the battle between the warrior, Loch, and the hero, Cuchulainn, Loch refuses to fight his opponent because he is clean-shaven (warriors were traditionally bearded) so Cuchulainn smears his chin with blackberry juice until it looks as if he has a beard and the battle commences. During the fight, the red-haired warrior goddess, Morrigan, appears three times to try to aid Loch. First she appears as a heifer, but Cuchulainn breaks its leg. Next she appears as an eel under his feet whilst the two men battle in running water but Cuchulainn stamps on her. Finally she appears as a wolf trying to seize his right arm but he puts out one of its eyes. Each time the Morrigan is defeated, Loch manifests a new wound. Cuchulainn finally defeats Loch with a magical spear called the **gae bolg** ('bellows-dart') made from the bones of a sea monster and having thirty barbs. There are other stories that tell of heroes who transform eels into powerful weapons and the **burach-bhaoi** ('wizard's shackle') was an enchanted eel with nine squinting eyes along its back that would drag horses under the water and drink their blood.

The eel teaches the power of holding on to wisdom and of not losing sight of the path ahead.

The seal

Seals were regarded as Otherworldly creatures and in Scotland and Ireland are called **selkies** ('seal people') who have the ability at certain times of year to come ashore, shed their skins and live for the night as humans. There are many tales of mortal men trying to steal the skins of beautiful selkie women in order to stop them returning to the sea but they nearly all end in tragedy.

Seals teach the power of song and its use in ceremony and healing.

The dolphin

Although this mammal does not appear in Celtic mythology, it is often seen in artwork, especially in depictions of sea deities, and was almost certainly seen as both an ally and guide in the Otherworld. The dolphin is one of the most powerful of all healing animals and can give one access to healing on all levels, physical, emotional and spiritual.

Magical creatures

The Celts frequently depict creatures that are magical and combine more than one attribute, such as the ram-headed serpent with hawk's wings and animals with human heads. These are linked to deities and probably show various totemic beasts combined in one representation. There are many stories of sea-monsters, dragons and serpents throughout Celtic literature and they appear as both allies and powerful destructive forces. Most are thought to inhabit the Otherworld, although amulets could be stolen from them and brought back to this world. One such amulet was the highly prized **Glainnaider** ('Snake Stone') worn by certain Druids. The stone was formed from the slime of coiling serpents and, once formed, was thrown in the air. The Druid had to catch it at that precise moment and flee for his life on a swift horse before the serpents attacked him. If such a creature appears to you in a vision or dream, look at all its symbolism for it is trying to teach you many things on many levels.

Working with animal medicine

What does it mean to work with animal medicine? Well, animals have a perspective upon life that is different to ours. They perceive a different reality, one that is forever seeking that place of balance and harmony. Nature always seeks balance, and animals, untarnished by complicated thinking, are part of that process. If an animal eats something that upsets its stomach, it naturally knows to seek out a specific herb to treat that ailment. It is so in touch with its intuition that it will go and eat exactly the correct therapeutic dose to solve the problem. What a powerful resource that would be to any human who could learn it. Every animal has resources or characteristics that we can learn from and as we learn, we become wiser and closer to balance and harmony.

Humans can communicate with and learn from animals but we have forgotten how. To the Celts it would have seemed unnatural and foolish not to communicate with animals. They understood that this would deny them the opportunity for great learning because they regarded animals and themselves as close relatives. In our modern state of arrogance we think we are so in advance of the animal kingdom that we have nothing to learn from them. How foolish this is! If a man cut himself off from all communication with his fellow man, we would judge him to be sick in some way and yet we do not realise our own sickness in our denial of the teachings animals have to give.

Our brains have different vibrations depending on what state of mind we are in. These vibrations are called brainwaves. In our normal waking state our brains produce *beta* waves and have a vibration of 14 to 34 Hz. As we become more relaxed, our brainwave patterns slow down to somewhere between 8 and 13 Hz and these are called *alpha* waves. In this state of mind we are daydreaming, meditating or imagining. The interesting thing is that the normal waking brainwaves of most animals are *alpha* waves. This means that if you want to communicate and connect with animal energies, you need to be in that daydream state. If you try to connect to the energies of animals using your conscious mind, you will not be able to make a true connection. It is only by simplifying and slowing your thinking that you can begin to understand the teachings and communications of the animal kingdom.

In Chapter Three, I related a story about an encounter I had with the fairy realm whilst meditating in a ring of mushrooms around a badger set. Well, after that experience I continued my walk in the woods still maintaining a daydream state of mind. As I was walking, a badger kept appearing in my mind. I have become used to such things so I asked the badger what it wanted. It replied that it had a gift for me and that I should follow its trail. It was then that I came across another badger set, hidden behind a thicket of hawthorn and hazel trees. As I entered the area, it was obvious that the set was not in current use. I sat down and opened my mind to whatever perceptions wished to enter. I sat, with my eyes open, bathing in badger energy. I could feel the energy of the badger all around me and my mind was filled with images of badgers. Then, as I dreamily looked around, my eyes were drawn to the roots of a hazel tree. I stared at them for a while when suddenly something came sharply into focus. There, hidden beneath an exposed root was a badger skull and as it came into focus, the badger in my mind said, 'I told you I had a gift for you and if you follow my trail I shall show you another.'

I love finding things like skulls and feathers. To me they are the most wonderful gifts from the creator. They allow me to easily make a connection with an animal whilst doing ceremony which I find both empowering and instructive. I was filled with joy at finding the skull and thanked the badger for its gift. I left an offering as a token of thanks and promised the badger that I would honour its gift to me by seeking to meditate with it and learn from its energy. I then continued on my walk, still with a strong sense of the badger close to me. I soon came across a badger trail and decided to follow it. You can recognise a badger trail because all the vegetation is pushed aside and this was confirmed by a pawprint in some soft mud.

As I walked, the badger was chattering in my mind telling me where to walk and look. Every time I thought I had lost the trail, the badger would tell me in my mind where to go and I would always quickly come across signs where badgers had been digging for roots to confirm I was on the right track. That day the badger led me a merry dance all through the woods. I went up and down hills and to parts of the wood I had not explored before. After a while the badger's promise of another gift came into my mind and at that precise moment I spotted something rolling down the hill I was traversing at the time. Then I heard the badger saying to me, 'There it is,' and so I followed the rolling object. When it stopped and I picked it up, I saw that it was a stone that I had obviously disturbed as I was walking, but as I looked at it I began to realise that it was no ordinary stone. It was silver-grey in colour and covered in indentations that looked like the burrowing of molluscs. It was a stone that had spent most of its life in the sea and the moment I picked it up I had images of water coming into my mind. How this stone came to be in the middle of a wood miles away from any coastline I have no idea, but I took it home and have kept it as one of my personal medicine stones.

Again, you may think that all this is just the product of an overactive imagination but, if this is so, was I led to the skull and the stone purely by chance? I think not. This story is just one of many incidents and interactions with animals that I have had over many years. I have been led to find all sorts of wonderful treasures in the woods and countryside just by allowing my mind to relax and my intuition to take over. What's more, I am often led to them by animals. Buzzards fly in front of me leading me to their beautiful feathers, deer appear to me before I am about to find a skull or an antler, and so on. It has happened to me so often now that I no longer question it. If I am walking in the woods and come to a junction, I often wait and look down each path for a sign. Invariably a crow will appear down one of the paths and that is the path I take. I have been led in this way on some wonderful walks and discovered all sorts of beauty, from rare wild herbs and orchids to remarkable trees, animal bones and stones. When I have walked consciously searching for treasures such as feathers and bones, I have found nothing. If I allow my ego to say to me, 'I want to find something on this walk,' then I find nothing. It is only when I walk with beauty, honour and respect expecting nothing more than the pleasure of being with Nature that I am rewarded with the most remarkable gifts. This is animal medicine.

Seven

THE POWER OF THE LAND

In the summer of 1999, *New Scientist* magazine published an article called 'The planet that hums' reporting on a discovery by two Japanese geophysicists, Naoki Suda and Kazunari Nawa, of an underlying hum made by the earth. This hum is a series of fifty or so notes crammed into two octaves with pitches ranging from two to seven millihertz. It is inaudible to the human ear being some sixteen octaves below middle C but it is there and no one knows where it comes from. They have ruled out seismic activity and at present can say only that it exists. The earth sings what to us is a discordant mass of notes, but sing it does. This is the first scientific evidence for what the Celts and other ancient civilisations knew thousands of years ago.

To the Celts the land upon which they lived was sacred, with each animal, plant and rock having its own vibration or song. Their minds were not tarnished with modern scientific closed thinking and I have no doubt that our ancestors could not only tune into these songs on a psychic level, but also used the energy of their own thought patterns and voices to interact with and influence these songs. There are stories of shamans moving stones the size of those that make up Stonehenge by singing to them. This may be beyond the imagination of most people but open your mind for a while to the possibility that everything has its own song or vibration.

This planet is full of special places with special songs that have been recognised as sacred sites for millennia. These are places where the healing energies of the earth rise to the surface and can be harnessed for the benefit of mankind. They include healing wells, mountains, sacred groves and a whole host of other magical places. We have all experienced the energy of a place at some time or other. Perhaps it was a church (remember, many were built on pre-Christian sacred sites), a forest or a beach, but wherever it was, there was something about the place that made it special. We are all sensitive to the atmosphere of such places but our education teaches us to ignore these feelings. Have you ever walked into a room and felt an atmosphere of disharmony that is so clear that no one even has to say anything for you to notice it. Or perhaps you have been to a sports match and sensed the excitement and passion of the crowd? If so, you are just sensing the song of the place, which has been created by the energies of the people. That same sense can be used to tune into the subtler vibrations of creation.

Everything and everyone has their own unique song. Places of negative energy sing a negative song as do people who hold on to anger, resentment and other inharmonious energies. When you feel 'out of sorts' what you are really feeling is out of tune. The road back to harmony can be found by reconnecting with the songs of the land. The Celts viewed all the land as sacred but certain places had an extra something about them, a song so sweet that it could inspire and bring back to harmony anything that had lost its own song. These places were used for healing and reconnecting with the creator so that those who heard the songs of these places could remember their own songs.

Stone circles and other pre-Celtic sites

It is an established fact that the ancient stone circles were built by pre-Celtic civilisations, but I have no doubt that the Celts, when they arrived in Britain and Ireland sensed the power of these places and utilised their energies for healing and connecting to the earth. Put out of your mind all thoughts of these circles being built by primitive cavemen who understood very little about the planet they lived on. Many of the ancient sites are orientated to the movement of the sun, moon and stars with such mathematical precision that we have only been able to think about the possibility of duplicating them since the invention of modern computers. The stone circle at Callanish in the Western Isles, for instance, appears at first sight to be a collection of randomly shaped stones in an imperfect circle and punctuated by rows of other randomly shaped stones. In fact the whole site is a complicated temple orientated to the movement of the sun, moon and stars. The Greek historian, Diordorus Siculus, is thought to be talking about Callanish when he speaks of a spherical temple in Britain where the moon 'dances continuously the night through from vernal equinox until the rising of the Pleiades.' What is more amazing is that if you stand by a certain stone on the dawn of the spring equinox, two of the circle stones that normally appear of random shape form a window that perfectly frames the rising sun. We still know comparatively little about these places of power but the more we study these ancient sites, the more we discover about their complexity.

If you visit any one of the hundreds of such sites dotted throughout Britain and Ireland you will begin to sense the power and sacredness of the land. Stonehenge and Avebury are the most famous but there are many other lesser-known sites that have a powerful magic about them. I remember visiting the Nine Stones in Dorset, England, some years ago to perform a ceremony with a group of friends. The site is right next to a main road and one would think that the sound of passing cars would be intrusive but the moment we entered the site it was as if we had walked through a doorway into another world. We lost all sense of time and spent about three hours there, although it seemed like only half an hour, and not once did we notice the sound of the traffic despite the fact that the road is frequently used both day and night. The song of the place is so strong that it repels all inharmonious sounds in the minds of those within its scared circle.

Whenever I visit such sites I am always struck with a sense of magic. When performing ceremonies at stone circles my companions and I have often felt the stones hum with a deep resonant note that vibrates to the very core of your being. I always leave these places with new insights and understandings, knowing that there is an energy about them that can have a profound effect on how you view the universe. Since I have been eating in harmony with the land I have felt these energies in a much more real and powerful way and now have no doubt that they are places of sacredness and power. Every year I try to take some time out to visit these ancient sites to experience their energy and listen to their songs. Sometimes I go with a group of friends and other times it is just Debbie and me. What we actually do at the site depends on how we perceive the energies of it and upon the voices of our intuition.

Some of the less well known sites I have visited have needed a great deal of work to clean them and make them ready for ceremony. Many have been overgrown with weeds or covered in litter and so often the work done is of a mainly physical nature. When you visit such a site, its song is masked but as you clean it so the song becomes louder and clearer. If the site is clean I may just sit and meditate to gain an understanding of the energy of the place and how best to work with it. Sometimes, even when alone, I perform a simple ceremony to honour the site and always feel a tangible change in atmosphere afterwards. It is as if the place comes alive; the more work that is put into a place, the more energised and powerful it becomes.

I make annual pilgrimages to Stonehenge and Avebury but a majority of the work I do is at less visited sites because I feel these need more attention. I believe that waking up the dormant sites not only honours the land, it also improves the energy of the whole area. Many stone circles have guardian spirits or powerful elemental energies and these need to be treated with honour and respect. There are those who fear these energies through their lack of understanding but I have found that, provided you work from a perspective of love and respect, you can do no harm and no harm can come to you.

Chambered long barrows, another pre-Celtic creation, have been seen by modern archaeologists as ancient burial grounds because human remains have been found in them but they were often much more than that. They were places of ceremony and initiation and I have had many profound experiences whilst visiting them. Remember that the Celts viewed death in a different way to us and performing ceremony whilst surrounded by the bones of your ancestors was regarded as a powerful way to get in touch with the ancient wisdom of the ancestors. The bones hold memories in the form of DNA that can be harnessed and learnt from by those who know how and stones are like record-keepers that hold a memory of every vibration they have ever come into contact with. The Celts regarded stones as the most ancient of all the spirit energies on this planet and the keepers of the most ancient and wisest of all teachings. Honouring and working with these ancient energies can give you the opportunity to gain rich understandings about yourself and the universe around you.

Standing stones and Celtic crosses

Long before the arrival of Christianity, there were sacred standing stones dotted throughout Celtic Britain, Ireland and Brittany. Again this was originally a pre-Celtic phenomenon and is thought to have had a variety of purposes. Some of the stones mark nodal points on the earth, similar to the acupuncture points that punctuate the energy pathways running throughout the body. The earth too has these pathways, known today as ley-lines but which in Celtic times were called dragon, serpent or fairy paths. At these special points the deep energies of the earth rise upward to the surface and the placing of a standing stone at these points amplifies that energy. In Britain such stones were generally of a moderate height of between ten and fifteen feet (3 to 5 m) high, but there are some in Brittany that are much taller, such as the Menhir of Kerloaz that stands over forty feet (13 m) high. Even that is said not to be its original height, the top being lost many years ago after a lightning strike.

Other standing stones were shaped in the form of a phallus and were placed to boost the fertility of both land and people. One such stone once stood in the centre of Avebury stone circle and was twenty-two feet (7 m) high, but was broken up for house building in the eighteenth century. All standing stones are thought to be representations of the *axis mundi* or 'world tree', connecting heaven and earth and were used regularly in ceremonies and rituals. The Celts adopted this practice marking their stones with ogham and knotwork. They also placed some as memorials to past heroes, kings and warriors and, though I have no evidence, I believe that in some cases the stone actually marks the burial spot. This would allow access to the wisdom and knowledge held within the bones of the buried person. Later, the Celts began to mark their stones with the sign of the Wheel of Life and thus the Celtic cross was born.

When Christianity arrived, many of these crosses were carved with Christian symbols and standing stones often had a cross placed on top of them. One has to remember that Celtic Christianity was very different from that of the Roman Church. Many of the Celtic saints were in fact Druids and shamans whose teachings of respect for oneself and creation fell perfectly in line with the original ethos of the early Christian church. It was only later when the Roman Christians became deluded with thoughts of world domination that the honour and respect was forgotten in favour of war and torture.

As the Celts changed from a nomadic to a more settled life-style, standing stones and crosses were erected in the centre of the community. These acted as focal points for ceremonies and meetings and were the precursors of the more modern Market Cross. Criminals were also tied to these crosses overnight, not as a punishment but as a cure. The Celts believed that by tying a criminal to a cross, he or she would spend the night connecting to the harmonising energies of the earth and many were said to be cured of their criminal tendencies in this manner. It may seem strange to tie criminals to what was regarded as a sacred object but this again demonstrates just how different the Celtic attitude to their fellow man was. Next time you visit an old market town with its original cross still standing, go and stand with your back against it for a while. Try to listen to its song and you may well gain a deeper understanding of the power of this practice.

To me, standing stones are places of power and healing. Whenever I visit an area with a nearby standing stone or cross, I try to visit it and leave a small offering at its base to honour and connect with the energies of the area. If I am feeling a little off-centre, I stand against it and meditate for a while until I feel balanced again and it really does work. If you visit any area with a standing stone or cross it is always good to make a connection with it and to honour the energies of the land you are walking upon. It gives you a link with the local energies that will enable you to gain a better understanding of the area and, in the more remote regions where locals can be suspicious of strangers, it actually appears to make them more accepting of you.

Healing wells and sacred springs

Water is essential for life and sources of natural water have been honoured and revered since earliest times. The Celts believed that these natural waters had many healing properties and each sacred well or spring had its own guardian energy that was honoured before water was drawn from it. Even many lakes and rivers had their own guardian spirits that were honoured in ceremony at certain times of the year. The names of many lakes, lochs and rivers throughout the Celtic lands are derived from the names of the Celtic deities that guarded them. Many Celtic artefacts have been found at such places. Hot springs, at Bath, for example, were utilised by the Celts long before the Roman invasion of Britain. The old Roman name for Bath, 'Aqua Sulis', acknowledges that the Celtic healing goddess Sulis was honoured there long before they arrived. This is confirmed by the Celtic coins that have been found at the bottom of the springs, probably left as votive offerings.

Healing wells and springs were particularly revered through-out the Celtic lands and there are many stories of miracles and healing associated with them. One such story relating to a well on Omey Island, just off the coast of Connemara in the west of Ireland, concerns Saint Feichin, the local saint who was probably a Druid, and his encounter with marauding Vikings. It is said that when the Vikings arrived on Omey, they decapitated Saint Feichin. Under normal circumstances this would have proved fatal but Saint Feichin picked up his own head, walked to the local well and, after dipping the head in it, placed it back upon his shoulders and was immediately restored.

In many parts there were annual pilgrimages to healing wells where a ceremony called **bowsenning** took place. It involved keeping a waking vigil by the well on the eve of a holy day and immersing oneself at dawn in the healing waters. Such ceremonies still take place today and in Castlekieran, County Meath, on the first Sunday after Lughnasadh, pilgrims approach the well of St. Ciarán at midnight by the light of torches to try and spot an elusive, magical trout that is said to inhabit it. Throughout Britain well-dressing ceremonies continue as an annual event although the church now carries out most of them. There are some very magical springs and wells. In the English city of Wells, seven springs feed the moat around the Bishop's Palace and nearby Glastonbury with its white and red healing wells. The waters of the white well are rich in calcium and those of the red well are rich in iron. Both wells surface within a few yards of each other and are used even today by many pilgrims and travellers. If you look on a good ordinance survey map, you will find wells and springs marked. You could decide to visit some — following your intuition will help you choose which ones — and you may also like to leave a small offering and partake of the waters. There are literally hundreds of forgotten or neglected wells that would welcome the honouring and attentions of humans again in return for their healing and rejuvenating waters.

Hill tops and high places

The Celts regarded hill tops and mountains as the sacred resting-places of the gods. Much of the folklore surrounding many of these sites has long been Christianised, with the devil being blamed for their formation rather than the Celtic deities. But some still retain their Celtic roots, the most famous of which is probably Glastonbury Tor. This unique hill in Somerset, England, was said to house one of the entrances to the Celtic Underworld and local legend tells of an encounter between St. Collen and Gwyn ap Nudd, king of the fairies.

St. Collen, a wandering monk/Druid was living as a hermit on top of the Tor and one day overheard two men talking about Gwyn. He warned them not to speak of such things because they were of the devil. The men warned him in return that he would soon meet Gwyn face to face. Shortly afterwards a messenger from Gwyn came to St. Collen requesting his presence in the fairy palace. Three times he refused to go, but on the fourth occasion he agreed and took with him a flask of holy water hidden under his cloak. He was taken to a secret door on the side of the Tor and found himself in a large hall where, before him, sitting on a golden throne, was Gwyn. Gwyn offered St. Collen food and drink but the monk refused both for fear of becoming enchanted because the offerings were of fairy origin. Instead, he sprinkled holy water all around and was immediately alone on the hillside. This is probably a retelling of a much older, pre-Christian tale and has much in common with other tales from Celtic mythology.

Another interesting feature of one or two sacred hills is the chalk figure. These gigantic landmarks are unique to Britain with some dating from as far back as 1000 BCE. The finest examples include the Cerne Abbas Giant, the Long Man of Wilmington and the Uffington White Horse. They were carved out of the hillside by removal of the shallow topsoil and grass, revealing the chalk underneath, and have been regularly tended by the local residents since their formation. Traditionally the scouring ceremonies took place every seven years and were accompanied by great merriment and feasting.

The scale of these figures is enormous and takes a great deal of time and a great many people to clean and scour them. The Cerne Abbas Giant stands some 170 feet (55 m) tall, holds a club that is 115 feet (37 m) long and has a phallus measuring 22 feet (7.2 m) whilst the Long Man of Wilmington is even taller at 231 feet (70.6 m). Close to the Cerne Abbas Giant is the wonderful healing well of St. Augustine, which is well worth a visit. Although dedicated to a male saint, the well has strong feminine energies that seem to complement the fertile masculinity of the Giant. In the local parish church at Wilmington is a huge ancient yew tree that has grown so large it needs to be supported by wooden beams and Uffington is surrounded by ancient places of power which are all connected by an ancient trackway called the

Ridgeway (see page 166). Many sacred places have more than one special attraction and it is perhaps the joint songs of trees, sacred wells, holy hills and other phenomena that makes these places so special and vibrant with the energies of creation.

Magical trees and sacred groves

As we have already seen, trees were highly venerated in Celtic times. They were the playgrounds of the fairy folk and home to the Green Man, the archetypal Celtic god of the plant kingdom. Just as Cernunnos was the universal Celtic lord of the animals, so the Green Man was lord of the forest. His image was often carved in wood and stone to decorate the outside of houses bringing in the woodland energies to the home. His face was usually portrayed as a collection of oak leaves and acorns but at other times it was an amalgamation of many different trees. Individual trees and collections of trees were also the homes of other gods and goddesses and the tree was seen as the original symbol of life. According to Celtic lore the first woman was created from a rowan tree and the first man from an alder.

The tree was not only a symbol of life, but also of death. Many trees embodied this in their annual shedding and re-growing of leaves: death into life and life into death. The wooden coffin was originally a hollowed-out tree trunk; the guardian spirit of the tree surrounded the bones of the deceased and would be a guide to the deceased in the Otherworld. It would then be traditional to plant a tree over the burial to mark and honour the spot and these can still be found throughout Britain and Ireland at the graves of bards and heroes. The planted tree was usually either a cutting of the original tree used to make the coffin or a plant grown from its seed. This was traditional, not only at graves, but also at the site of any tree that had come to the end of its life. The Celts believed that if they planted the offspring of a tree in its place when it died the guardian spirit would remain to be honoured and learnt from. The holy thorn at Glastonbury is an example where a sacred tree planted nearly two thousand years ago still has many of its offspring dotted around the town.

Trees that grew in an unusual form or those that had been struck by lightning were especially venerated by the Celts. They would often be the focal point for ceremonies in honour of the Green Man and other deities. And if wood was taken from any tree for magical use or if the counsel of the tree's guardian spirit was being sought, the tree would be honoured with an offering.

Trees growing together, especially those grouped on the tops of hills, were especially favoured by the Druids for their ceremonies. Of greatest distinction were oak groves. The circle of trees was symbolic of the circle of life with four trees at the cardinal points representing the four elements. Groves were often dedicated to local deities and utilised by all the local inhabitants for ceremonies. However, some were regarded as the homes of dark and powerful elemental energies and would only be approached by a solitary shaman or Druid at certain nodal times of the year.

According to Celtic lore the forest was regarded as the favourite haunt of the fairy folk, especially forests containing thorn trees. This was extended to include single thorn trees growing on hillsides and those growing by sacred wells or springs. When water was drawn from the well an offering was often tied to the nearest tree to honour both the guardian of the well and the fairy folk. This tradition continues at some wells today, for example, at the white well at Glastonbury, where trees are still adorned with coloured ribbons and other offerings.

The tree was also the symbol of inspiration for bards and a rare example of one such bardic tree is the Caerwys Tree, a sycamore in North Wales. Other trees came to symbolise towns and families, such as the famous oaks of Sevenoaks and those still displayed on the coats of arms of many old families with Celtic roots.

The wonderful thing about trees is that almost wherever you go in the world you find them growing. In many of the towns, cities, villages and hamlets of the Celtic lands you can still find ancient trees and their offspring. Whenever I go walking in a forest or woodland I am always amazed by the variety of shape and form of different trees. Every once in a while I have an encounter with a remarkable tree that leaves me speechless, in awe of its magic and the beauty of its song. They are remarkable for so many reasons, some because they are very ancient, others because of their adornment with fungi. These often look like whole villages in miniature and are fascinating to look at whilst allowing your imagination to run free. Trees are whole universes in themselves and, even after many years of walking amongst them, still such sights never fail to impress me.

Caves and caverns

Caves and caverns were often used by the Celts as places of initiation. Entering a cave was like walking into the womb of Grandmother Earth and was symbolic of death and rebirth. Caves were access points to the Underworld and were often the dwellings of dark and powerful spirits which later made them feared as the habitations of demons. However, these dark energies were regularly sought out by shamans and Druids for their deep and ancient wisdoms and there are many tales of men and women emerging from caves having gained a new talent after being taken by these spirits to the Underworld. In Somerset, England, at Cheddar and Wookey Hole are some of the most spectacular cave systems in Britain and both sets of caves have strong Celtic connections. They have in the past been used as burial chambers, hermits' lodges and ceremonial centres as shown by the host of archaeological finds and local folklore.

Though chambered long barrows were frequently used by the Celts for initiatory purposes, they also built subterranean chambers and tunnels for similar purposes. These appear throughout the Celtic lands and show great variety of form and structure. Some are single passageways leading to an end chamber whilst others are more complex with side chambers and sudden changes in ground level. They are usually trenches dug out of the earth and capped with flagstones and are generally called *souterrains*, but they have various local names, the best known of which is the Cornish 'fogou'. Caves and souterrains are well worth visiting and experiencing because they have a unique energy about them. They are often cold, dark and confining which can bring up many fears in people but if these fears are faced and let go of, much can be learned from them. I find such places very evocative and spending time meditating in a cave, especially at night, always inspires visions.

Holy islands

Islands held a special significance to the Celts. Whether small outcrops of land in the middle of a lake or a huge island off the sea, all in Britain and Ireland were regarded as sacred. The Celtic Otherworld is often described as a series of islands and, because islands are cut off from the mainland, they were held to be cut off from the influences of men and thus under the care and control of Otherworldly beings. Many were sacred to specific deities, such as the Isle of Man whose name originally related to the Celtic sea god Manannan Mac Lir, and they were usually seen as independent of mainland government. Many islands had their own parliament and some even had their own queen or king who was usually the eldest and wisest of the inhabitants.

Druidic hermits would often live alone on a deserted island and later monks and nuns took over these holy islands, Iona, for example, building churches and centres of ceremony on them. Many had sacred springs and shrines dedicated to local deities as well as standing stones and Celtic crosses. Mainland folk would make pilgrimages to these islands for ceremonies and to seek the council of the wise men and women that lived on them. Most large islands such as Anglesey, Iona and Skye had permanent spiritual communities living on them whilst the smaller islands inhabited by solitary holy men were known as 'priests' islands'. Any island with the word **Papa** in its name was a priest's island and these can still be found in the Scottish Shetland and Orkney isles. Most have a rich and complex mythology surrounding them with tales of epic encounters between Celtic holy men and women and Otherworldly beings. Many of these holy people have become local saints and the islands they inhabited now often bear their names.

According to legend, the final resting-place of Merlin is a mystical island off the coast of Britain. It is said that he travelled there with nine attendant bards and the thirteen magical treasures of Britain. These treasures were enchanted gifts from the gods and each had their own unique powers:

1. Dyrnwyn ('White Hilt'), the sword of Rhydderch the Generous
2. The Hamper of Gwyddno Garanhir
3. The Horn of Bran
4. The Chariot of Morgan the Wealthy
5. The Halter of Clydno Eiddyn
6. The Knife of Llawfronedd the Horseman
7. The Cauldron of Dyrnwch the Giant
8. The Whetstone of Tudwal Tydglyd
9. The Coat of Padaen Red-Coat
10. The Crock of Rhygenydd the Cleric
11. The Dish of Rhygenydd the Cleric
12. The Chessboard of Gwenddolau ap Ceidio
13. The Mantle of Arthur of Cornwall.

The loss of the treasures symbolises the loss of the old knowledge to Christianity. They will not re-emerge until the old ways of honouring and respecting the land have been restored.

It is popularly believed that the island where Merlin rests is the aptly named Bardsley island off the westernmost point of Caernarvonshire but, as the legend goes, Merlin is hidden within an invisible glass castle and so the many treasure-seekers who have scoured every inch of this island have always left disappointed.

Ancient tracks and the sacred land

Undertaking a long journey in Celtic times was a potentially perilous pursuit. Not only might you be crossing the lands of other, perhaps hostile tribes, you might also face ferocious animals, have to cross wild fords and rivers and climb long, steep hills. Virtually every journey provided obstacles to be negotiated and hazards to be aware of. Routes would need to be planned and if the journey lasted more than a few days, as most did, you would need to find sources of clean water and fresh food. This was especially important in winter when many water sources were frozen and food was scarce.

The Celts had an intrinsic knowledge of the land and their myths and legends, which they were taught from childhood, provided vital information about the nature of the land. A Celt would know exactly where the best routes and the purest springs were in any area, even if he had never visited it before. There were no maps and no signposts — so how did he gain this knowledge?

The myths and legends of the Celts were many things on many levels. They were parables and teachings, giving lessons about life and telling the true nature of the universe. But they were also maps showing the locations of special trees, stone circles, sacred springs and so on. When a bard, the Celtic storyteller, was learning his stories and poems, he had to learn them exactly, word for word. When retelling them, he never once deviated from the original tale. He embellished no detail nor left any out because every word had significance and meaning. A tale of a hero or heroine would contain specific details of the area in which it was set. A hero would perhaps be walking along a known path and would come across a magical tree. This would mark out a remarkable tree at a specific place and act as a signpost to anyone taking that path in the future. In the tree might be a magical crow that instructed the traveller to walk to the east where he would find an enchanted spring. The crow, being associated with death, would be a warning: to fail to listen to its wisdom could result in death. If the tale took place in winter, this might be the only unfrozen source of natural water for many days and not to take on supplies from it could prove fatal to any traveller venturing along that path in winter.

Every detail of the tale would contain an exact description of an area showing sources of food and water, resting-places, hazards and so on. If a Celt were travelling anywhere in the known lands, he would be able to recall a tale that would guide him through that land. When a hazard such as a wild river needed to be negotiated, he would know the precise location of a local tree-spirit or river goddess who could be called upon to guide and empower his crossing. He would leave an offering of some kind to honour the spirit before crossing and would leave another offering of thanks at the next resting-place. Sadly, much of this knowledge has been lost but it was once how all ancient people of the world guided themselves. The Australian Aborigines and one or two of the more remote rainforest tribes are the only people today who still retain this type of knowledge.

The **fili**, one of the orders of Druidry, spent twelve years in training memorising 250 primary stories and 100 secondary stories. These provided 350 maps which included every necessary detail, such as landmarks, dangers, resting-places, all perfectly noted in the memory of the storyteller. If you were to embark on a journey, you would seek out a **filidh** (the singular of fili) and ask him or her to tell you the tales of the area you were travelling through. The fili were walking atlases with guidebooks to every village, woodland and moor for hundreds of miles around. Today that would be like driving with maps to the whole country, including town and city street plans, at the ready. Again, this is another talent our ancestors possessed that we can only emulate with computers. Before in-car route planners, the idea of taking 350 maps with you on a journey would seem preposterous, but in Celtic times, if you had an **ollamh filidh** (the highest of the seven grades of fili) travelling with you, that's the number of maps you had at your instant disposal.

Many of the ancient trackways are called dragon or serpent paths because they form part of the earth's energy matrix. These paths, or ley-lines as they are sometimes called, are paths connecting sacred sites and holy springs. One such path runs from St. Michael's Mount in the far west of Cornwall all the way across southern Britain to Bury St. Edmunds taking in major sacred sites like Glastonbury and Avebury and a whole host of minor sites. Many of these minor sites are now churches dedicated to St. Michael, a dragon-slaying saint, or St. Mary, the Christianised version of the Celtic earth goddess. The path also takes in many megalithic sites, making it clear that these invisible energy pathways were also known to the pre-Celts.

Another ancient trackway is the Ridgeway that runs through Oxfordshire and Berkshire ending at Avebury. It takes in many wonderful sacred sites, including Uffington Castle (an Iron-Age hill fort), the Uffington White Horse and Wayland's Smithy (a megalithic tomb built on top of an earlier long barrow). If you walk along this path you can sense history all around you. The Celts and their predecessors walked this track on their pilgrimages to Avebury, one of the largest ceremonial sites in Britain, and sites along the route, such as Wayland's Smithy near Uffington have a quiet sacredness about them that gives one a real sense of how our ancestors viewed the land. Many tracks are winding rather than straight but, if you think that straight roads were a Roman invention, think again. A visit to Rough Tor in north Cornwall dispels this myth — if you stand on top of the Tor and face towards Tintagel, you can see an ancient Celtic road leading straight from the Tor directly towards the ancient Celtic village with its castle and sacred cave called Merlin's Cave. This is just one of many perfectly straight tracks linking sacred sites, many of which are pre-Celtic in origin.

In Celtic times much of Britain was covered in woodland and the paths through these woods were often referred to as fairy paths. They had a very different quality to the dragon paths meandering here and there so, if one was not clear about which route to take, one could easily become lost, especially if the fairy mist descended. There are many tales of men forgetting where they are meant to be going after following a beautiful fairy woman or becoming disorientated in an enchanted mist and ending up in the Otherworld. And the likelihood of this was increased if they had not been respectful by leaving an offering to ensure safe passage. Such tales act as parables showing the importance of honouring and respecting the land you are travelling. Nowadays, with our cars and other modern means of transport, we have lost touch with this concept and thus with our connection to the land.

Reconnecting with the land

Wherever you are, in a town, city or the country, you can form a personal relationship with the land. Even the animals and trees

sing their songs in the parks and avenues of cities whilst, beneath
the concrete buildings and tarmac streets, the earth hums her never-
ending serenade. Connecting with the plants and animals of the
place where you live will give you a real sense of belonging and
can provide many insights and understandings. Many now heavily
populated areas were originally centres of sacredness and a little
research into the local mythology of an area can often provide
clues as to the location of energy centres in that area. If you are
travelling in Britain, an Ordnance Survey map of the region
usually shows the location of springs, pre-historic sites and other
special places and it is worth taking time out to visit these places
and to honour them with a simple ceremony.

It is also good to find a special place in your locality where
you can regularly go and reconnect with the energy of the land.
It might be a local park, a single tree, a church, hilltop or forest. If
the area is neglected, you might wish to re-activate its energies by
clearing it of debris and litter and perhaps constructing a simple
altar from local materials. I have a small area of ancient woodland
near to where I live and within it stands a very old solitary yew.
When I first came across it I was struck by its beauty and magic.
The area underneath its canopy had an atmosphere that was dis-
cernibly different from the rest of the wood. I have since brought
friends and patients to visit it and everyone has noticed it. There
was a quiet calm there and as I placed my hands upon its huge
trunk, I felt a wave of warmth travel through my hands, up my arms
and through my whole body. I thanked the tree for its gentle energy
and promised to honour it whenever I visited the woodland.

Since then I have visited it regularly and have found that the
tree speaks through my intuition showing me how to honour this
place and make it even more sacred. One day I was instructed to
make a simple altar with a piece of wood I found whilst walking
there and I now use it to make offerings of herbs and salt to
honour the tree. If I ever feel in need of some clarity of mind or
healing of the body, I go and visit that yew and each time I come
away renewed and refreshed. The more work I do there, the more
powerful it becomes for me. I am currently in the process of

constructing a stone circle around it and although now I visit it as a preparation for ceremonies I carry out elsewhere, soon it will become a ceremonial site in its own right. I do not know if this place had significance and sacredness in the past but, with my energy and that of the many friends who have visited it with me, I have made it so today.

If you cannot find a sacred site close to where you live, create your own. When Debbie and I first moved to our home in Somerset, the garden had been very neglected with parts of it untouched for over thirty years. Over the years since we have been here, we have turned it into our own, personal, sacred site. As we were deciding what to do with it, we sought guidance from the mature trees that surrounded it and were led to make it our primary place of ceremony. Every time we walk out of our door, we reconnect with the energy of the land and by regularly gathering with friends to honour the land in ceremony, that connection has now grown in power and strength. It has become a tranquil haven of peace and healing and has given us a real sense of belonging. Whenever we return from travelling, the energy of the house and garden welcomes our return so that we are able to quickly relax and get our energies back into harmony with our home. It is difficult to describe it but there is the feeling of a 'Welcome Home' party that raises our spirits and fills our hearts with joy. This is the power of honouring the land. It reaps rich rewards that can improve every aspect of your life and well-being. To some people it is the fantasies of a deluded mind, but people who think of me in that way are also full of sadness and inner turmoil. Debbie and I have created our haven and it serves us well in the real world improving the quality of our lives and those we share it with. People only think this is fantasy because they have not learnt how to create such a positive reality in their own lives. But it is possible for everyone to have this magic in their lives if they choose to. It just takes a little time, effort and a willingness to be open to learning from anything and everything. To hear the song of the land or any sacred site within the land takes only practice and belief. If you do not believe in the song, you will never hear it, but if you open your mind you will understand that everything really does have its own song, including you. As you walk your path of destiny and if you do so with honour and respect, creation will sing to you every day its beautiful song of healing and harmony and, as it does, so will the power and beauty of your own song grow.

Eight

RESPECT AND THE POWER OF CEREMONY

The tribal society was primarily one of peace and acceptance, where violence had its place only as a last resort against invaders who came with aggression rather than in friendship, seeking to dominate rather than co-operate.

Celtic society was founded upon respect, not only for creation, but also for all beings. Everyone's uniqueness was celebrated and encouraged rather than frowned upon and suppressed as in modern society. The Celtic tribal system meant that every member of the tribe was respected and had a part to play in the community. Everyone had their own teachings and lessons, whether young or old, and all individuals were allowed to express themselves in whatever manner they felt was appropriate, provided it harmed no one.

The elders of the tribe were highly revered for their wisdoms and teachings and were often the primary educators of the young. The young were honoured because of their innocence — this too can teach volumes to those who understand its value. If you were unusual in any way, whether through character or physical or mental handicap, you were regarded as special because of your unique perspective and were recognised as a rich source of understanding and enlightenment. Homosexuals and transvestites were embraced with the same love and acceptance as any other person and were often asked to play important roles in ceremonies because of their understanding of both masculine and feminine.

Above all, though, it was women that were most honoured and respected in Celtic society because the Celts understood the power of women in a way we have long since lost. Before the arrival of the church and its patriarchal dominance, men and women were regarded as equal — neither sex was regarded as better or worse, weaker or stronger than the other. Each had its strengths and wisdoms and the tribal community was seen as an opportunity for both sexes to learn from one another. There was no stereotyping and the tribal structure allowed everyone to follow their path of destiny without fear of opposition or ridicule. There were male and female warriors, Druids, cooks, weavers, bards, musicians and every other type of craftsperson. Each individual followed their own intuition and instinct. Because everyone lived and ate in harmony with creation, the tribe remained balanced. There were never too many of one craft and not enough of another, the tribe naturally found its own internal balance. Many people learnt several crafts so that when extra hands were needed in one area people from other crafts could lend a hand. Many activities, such as sowing and harvesting, were carried out by every member of the tribe and most ceremonies involved everyone.

There was however one aspect of women that set them apart from the men in Celtic culture and that was menstruation. Women were seen as the living embodiment of creation, going through the process of life, death and rebirth every month in their menstrual cycle. In Celtic times, because everyone lived and ate in harmony with creation, the women were in phase with the moon and women all generally ovulated and menstruated at the same time. When women had their moon-time they separated themselves from the other members of the tribe, not because it was regarded as an unclean time, quite the opposite, it was a holy time. A woman in her moon-time was regarded as most holy and sacred because the Celts believed that, when a woman bleeds, the downward energy of her menstruation makes her thoroughly grounded. This in turn gives her access to high spiritual realms of wisdom that were not accessible to men.

When the women of the tribe had their moon-time, they would go to a sacred grove or spring and set up a lodge there so that they could gather together and share insights. It was a time when they could discuss matters of importance to the tribe because their unique combined energies at that time gave them access to high spiritual wisdom that could bring solutions and understandings to difficulties and problems.

The ancient words for menstruation also meant things such as sacred, goddess, spirit and supernatural and one of the Celtic names for menstrual blood was **dergflaith**, which means 'red sovereignty'. To wear red dye upon the body meant that the goddess had chosen you as a king and the Celtic word **ruadh** meant both 'red' and 'royal'. Thomas the Rhymer, a famous Celtic magician was, according to legend, told by the Fairy Queen to lay his head upon her lap where she had 'a bottle of claret wine'. This is a synonym for menstrual blood — the word claret meant 'enlightenment'. Clearly the Celts had an understanding of the mysteries and power of woman that we seem to have lost. I believe that if we could regain this and learn to respect again the sacred power of woman, we would be able to restore balance in the modern world.

Behind every powerful man there is an even more powerful woman — there is much truth in this saying. But I believe that by trying to compete with men at the expense of their higher spiritual wisdom, many women have given away their power. Nowadays women are expected to work regardless of whether they are bleeding or not and are often looked down upon both by men and women if their period causes a display of emotion. To all women I say it is time to reclaim your power and holiness by honouring this sacred time each month. To all men I say it is time to learn to respect this time in women — not doing so is not only disrespectful to women, it is also disrespectful to yourself.

Somehow we need to change the way we run our lives so that women can once again meet together at these times to share and honour one another. I am not saying that all women should give up their jobs so that they can be free at these times, but they should at least take some time out to honour their own sacredness at their moon-time. It is no coincidence that when women spend time together, their menstrual cycles will gradually fall into the same phase. It is one of the wonders of creation that allows women to gain both wisdom and power.

The reason many women have problems at their bleeding time is because they have lost respect for themselves. Your body is your temple and should be treated as such. This means eating natural foods, not synthetic products. So many processed foods contain oestrogen-like chemicals that unbalance the female hormonal system. Furthermore, the contraceptive pill has taken women still further away from their natural connection. One of the biggest confidence tricks played on women by men was the contraceptive pill. It was marketed as a road to freedom for women where once and for all women would have power over whether they conceived or not. On the contrary, I believe it has been a road to slavery, unbalancing the delicate internal chemistry of women, leading them to have many health problems in later life. The prime reason why many women have problems with their cycles is that they come into regular contact with synthetic hormones (either through contraception or food) and eat an unbalanced diet. My partner, Debbie, is living proof that when a women eats and lives in harmony with the land, she bleeds for three days only and during that time has access to understandings and wisdom that are humbling to witness.

Women do not need to compete with men; they are already on a higher spiritual plane. When a woman lives a balanced life she knows her body so well that she can tell exactly where she is in her cycle and can practice natural birth control because she knows her fertile times and her safe times. I tell my women patients that if, during their fertile times, their men are not willing to wear contraception, not only are the men being selfish, they are also being disrespectful to the temples that are the women's bodies. Any woman who allows a man to have unprotected sex with her against her better judgement and in order to please him is being disrespectful to herself and giving away her power. If women can once again learn to command respect, the imbalance between men and women that pervades modern society will become a thing of the past. Men have often ridiculed women through their fear and lack of understanding of the power and sacredness of the menstrual cycle and this needs to stop once and for all.

It is women who hold the true power and if both sexes can learn to have respect for this power, both can benefit in strength and wisdom. One of the things that I, as a man and practising shaman, have been led to search for is a true understanding of this power of women. Many men think that to respect a woman is a sign of weakness and that allowing a woman to hold on to her power will weaken them. How wrong they are! When man and woman come together with mutual honour and respect, both grow continually in power, wisdom and understanding. It takes a strong man to respect his woman and to be humble enough to listen to her wisdom and it takes a strong woman to teach her man to better understand her sacredness and power. Because women have access to higher realms of understanding, it is women who always lead the way in a balanced society. Debbie empowers my every action and word and without her I would not be writing this book. She does not weaken me, on the contrary I am empowered by her because she continually challenges me to look within myself and discover in me that which she already understands. I have needed to learn to be open to admitting my weaknesses and to be shown how to turn them into strengths. In that process the only part of me that has lost power is my ego. But as my ego has relinquished its power, my true spiritual self has been able to grow so that Debbie and I have a life of mutual respect and learning.

Ultimately the only way we will learn to respect one another is by first learning to respect ourselves. Eating and living in harmony with creation goes a long way towards this, but the Celts also understood the power of ceremony as a means of cementing that connection with Nature and of teaching respect. Human beings naturally run their lives in a ceremonial and ritualistic manner. We each have our individual rituals in day-to-day life, such as how we wash, dress and eat, but we have forgotten the potential power of these rituals to boost our self-respect and connection to creation. Washing is much more than a means of physically cleaning the body, it is an opportunity to cleanse body, mind and spirit of all negativity so that you start each day fresh and free of the encumbrances of the past. The colours you wear have a vibration that affects your own vibration and once you tune into this power you can dress for power and protection. The intent you put into your food preparation again has a marked effect on the nutritional quality of that food and so on.

Throughout this book I have talked about honouring and respecting the land. This can be done in many different ways. One of the simplest ways to do this is to honour the seven directions every morning. On rising, why not go outdoors and greet the seven directions as you feel appropriate? This may simply involve facing each of the directions and saying a simple prayer, or you may wish to perform a more elaborate ceremony. Below is an example of how you might like to greet the seven directions each morning.

Face the East and raising your arms towards that direction say:

Welcome Spirits of the East and honour to Grandfather Sun. I call upon the element of Air to instruct and inspire me. May I draw to myself this day the energies and lessons I need to empower me on my path of destiny. I honour all the feathered beings and thank them for their sweet song and gentle teaching. Help me to better understand their messages of peace and healing.

Turn to the South:

Welcome Spirits of the South and honour to all my relations [which means all humans and other living creatures]. I call upon the element of Fire to allow me to express clearly my destiny and to fuel my intuition. I honour all creatures of the land and ask that they will show me by their example how to follow a path of harmony. Help me to shine with light and beauty and to always seek truth.

To the West:

Welcome Spirits of the West and honour to the elemental energies of the gods. I call upon the element of Water to uplift and purify my body, mind and spirit and to fill me with unconditional love for all creation. I honour all creatures of the water and ask them to show me balance and gentleness. Feed my imagination and allow me to rise above all obstacles and difficulties.

Then turn to the North and say:

Welcome Spirits of the North and honour to the dark goddess. I call upon the element of Earth to ground me and fill me with the power of determination. Teach me more of the dark mysteries of the universe and inspire me to seek wisdom and understanding within myself. I honour the stone beings and ask that they will teach me their ancient ways so that I may die to all that is negative and be reborn into all that is positive.

Raise your eyes and arms to the heavens and say:

Welcome Grandfather Sky and all good spirits that dwell in other realms. Watch over me and guide me on my path and may the power of the moon teach me to embrace change and adversity with joy. Activate my higher spiritual consciousness that I may better understand my true purpose in life and fulfil that purpose with pleasure.

Kneel down, placing your hands flat upon the earth:

Welcome Grandmother Earth, she who sustains all life and allows me to walk upon her body. Honour to all plant energies and to the land of fairy. Teach me to walk always with honour and respect both for myself and all creation. I thank you for the gifts of food and nourishment you will give to me this day and ask that I be shown how best to repay this energy in a true and respectful way.

Finally place your hands over your heart or solar plexus and say:

Welcome Creator, Great Spirit, Great Mystery and honour to the spark of creation you have placed within me. May it shine with beauty and may I never cease in my search for balance and harmony in all things.

After this you may choose to face one direction, whose power you particularly feel drawn to and meditate for a while, allowing the energies you have just honoured to give you insight and under-standing. Simple ceremonies like this set your intent for the day to be respectful towards yourself and others and, if practised regularly, will dramatically change your life and the manner in which you perceive it.

Another way to make a stronger connection with creation is to construct an altar. An altar is a place where you can focus your mind and energies and it can act as a focal point when meditating or sending out healing thoughts and prayers. It does not necessarily need to be elaborate but I have found that, although most people begin with a simple altar, it grows over time into a magical mixture of many and varied beautiful things. You might like to mark the four cardinal directions with stones or small crystals or you could repre-sent the four elements with salt (Earth), incense (Air), a candle (Fire) and a bowl or small glass bottle of water (Water) arranged in a circle. We have several altars in our house of various shapes, con-tent and size. Some of the people who visit our home do not even recognise them as altars because to the ordinary individual they just appear to be a nice display of ornaments and trinkets.

Whenever I go walking, I find things such as feathers, nuts and stones catching my eye. I always get a sense of whether they want to come home with me or not and if they do they are usually placed upon one of our altars. I collect things throughout the seasons that I use to decorate my personal altar, such as leaves, twigs, berries and nuts. I find that these help me to connect with the turning wheel of the year. I try to take only those things I find fallen on the forest floor although I will take a single blossom or fruit from a tree if I feel led to. This is always done with honour and respect asking the plant's permission and leaving an offering (usually some salt or tobacco). I only take where I find abundance and never pick a solitary wild flower or fruit. In February I will take a single blackthorn flower and place it in a bowl of spring water on my altar and will do the same with the hawthorn in May. In March it may be a gorse flower and in the autumn and winter an acorn, chestnut, sloe, a sprig of holly or a piece of mistletoe. As each season passes and new things are brought in, the old is offered to the sacred fire of the next festival in a perpetual cycle of death and rebirth. The forest always reveals unusual and beautiful things, especially in the rain when the energy and whole atmosphere changes. Dull sticks take on new looks as the ornate grain in the wood is highlighted by the wet, and stones shine and sparkle, calling out to be picked up and listened to.

I quite often find something in the woods that I am clearly told has to stay in the energy of the wood. A stone will call out to be picked up and as I am walking with it images and thoughts will enter my mind as the stone speaks to me. Invariably once we have finished our 'conversation', I am told by my intuition to leave the stone in the woods. I often leave such things on my woodland altar so that I can reconnect with their energy the next time I enter the woods. Once, on the eve of the autumn equinox last year I was walking in the woods and I found lots of amazing treasures. First, I found three white pheasant feathers, then I found the wings of a crow. This seemed very poignant, especially on the eve of the day when the powers of the darkness take ascendancy. Everything I found that day had some significance to the festival I was going to celebrate that evening but I was clearly told that none of it was to travel home with me. Instead, I took them all to my woodland altar and decorated it to honour the trees and the woodland's many gifts. As I sat there and meditated I was given a vision of exactly the form that evening's ceremony should take. That evening Debbie and I gathered with friends and had a wonderful celebration together with a Celtic sweatlodge followed by a feast of seasonal foods. I was given the words to say in my prayers and shown teachings to impart. I cannot explain it adequately, but these experiences form an interconnected web of insights and inspirations that make our gatherings magical and enlightening experiences. When you walk with beauty and honour, creation rewards you in many wonderful ways.

A really nice way to create a sacred space is to build a stone circle. It does not have to be particularly big — I have a small one made of tiny crystals on an altar in my treatment room. We also have a simple circle made of four stones around our fire-pit where we build our sacred fires at festival times and on occasions when the energy of the fire is called for. Stone circles can come in all sizes with anything from four to over forty stones. You can use stones of an appropriate size to mark the four cardinal directions or the eight Celtic fire festivals. Whenever I construct a stone circle, I ask the stones themselves where they want to be placed and then follow the voice of my intuition as the stone speaks through it. I have made thirteen-stone circles honouring the thirteen tree months and fifteen-stone circles marking the seven directions and the eight fire festivals. Sometimes a stone will hold a single symbolism and at other times two or more. For instance, I might have three stones in the North (one to represent the cardinal direction, one to represent Earth and one to represent Yule) or I may have only one (representing North, Earth and Yule). It really depends on how the circle unfolds and how I am led by my intuition and the teachings of the nearby stones, plants and trees.

Stone circles are a representation of the Wheel of Life and are ideal for making a semi-permanent sacred place. They can be made anywhere, in gardens, forests, on hilltops or beaches. But before constructing such a circle there are several things that will help to make the energy of the place more conducive to ceremonial work. Whether you are constructing a permanent stone circle or a temporary one for a single ceremony, there are certain things that I have found help to prepare the place and also your mind. The circle is a representation of the Wheel of Life and, like the echo, whatever thoughts and intents you put into it will come back to you many times over. Making a sacred circle is not complicated and anyone can do it. There is no right or wrong way to do it and there are no rules. What I give you now are some of the insights and understandings I have gained from making ceremonial circles, but they are guidelines, not hard and fast rules. In an ever-changing universe one has to be always ready to embrace change and, although you might intend to follow my guidelines word for word, I guarantee that something will enter your mind that changes it slightly. This is good because it places your own unique energy in the ceremony. The following is a guideline for making a temporary ceremonial circle but the same preparation goes into constructing a permanent stone circle.

Creating a sacred circle for ceremony

The first thing to do when creating any circle is to make sure both you and the area you are working at are cleansed of all negative energies. You can do this in a variety of ways — sweeping with a birch broom or goose feather or cleansing with smoking herbs, such as sage or woodruff, or incense. As you do this visualise all negative energies either dispersing or being transmuted into positive energies. You might like to say a simple prayer at this time, such as:

> Grandmother Earth, I call upon you and the energies of the land to make this place sacred. I come here for the good of all creation and invite only what is good into this place.

Next, make sure your energy is well grounded by standing, kneeling, sitting or lying on the ground and imagining roots growing from your body deep into the earth. This will stop you from becoming vulnerable to fear or losing your clarity during the ceremony. Really try to feel your strong connection to Grandmother Earth and tune into her hum on a psychic level.

You can now cast your circle using salt, oatmeal, flower petals, stones, tobacco or whatever else feels appropriate. Cast in a sunwise (clockwise) direction using your right hand so that you remain outside of the circle. You can begin the circle at whatever place you feel appropriate and depending upon which energy you wish to focus. When you have cast nearly all the circle and have only a doorway left, enter the circle and then close it. This now forms an invisible seal holding the positive energies you create within the circle and all negative influences outside. As you are casting the circle you might wish to sing a simple song, hum a tune or say a simple prayer:

> Great Spirit, Grandmother Earth, I cast this circle in a sacred manner
> with reverence to all creation and to honour all life.

Once you have done this you can call into the circle whatever positive spirits and energies you feel drawn to. These can be plant, tree, animal or stone energies, spirit guides, deities or whatever feels good and right. You might like to create a simple invocation:

> North, East, South and West
> I ask this circle to be blessed.
> Earth below me, sky above,
> Creator fill this place with love.

Or you might like to call upon specific energies to bring to you resources or talents that you are currently seeking in your life:

> I call upon the energies of the boar to bring me strength and endurance
> and of the willow to show me flexibility.

Whatever energies you ask for they should be called with honour and respect and their presence should never be demanded nor commanded, but all prayers should take the form of gentle requests. This is because the human mind does not always have the ability to see the big picture and sometimes the energies that you call upon are not actually all appropriate to be with you. If you call them gently, those energies that are needed will come and those that are not will not. If however you begin demanding that energies appear or commanding them to do things for you that are not for the good of all, you are getting into very dangerous waters. Everything in ceremony should be done with love and beauty and the ego needs always to be kept under firm control.

Once you have called upon whatever energies you feel are appropriate, it is good to honour those energies with a simple song or chant and then to raise the power of the circle by moving gently or dancing to the rhythm of a song, chant, rattle or drum. As you feel the energy build, you might naturally increase in tempo, volume or complexity of sound, especially if there are several of you taking part in the ceremony. Follow your intuition singing a song or humming a tune from your heart. It does not have to be in tune, it just has to be sung with respect. Let your whole body become a moving prayer or song that rises from the depths of your soul and is expressed via the heart. Whether you laugh, cry, shout or dance, you should always follow your intuition, remembering that as long as you come from a place of love and respect, you can do no harm.

You will probably feel the energy reach a crescendo and then slowly calm as the energy reaches a higher level of vibration. It is difficult to describe it but once you feel it for yourself you will know what I mean. At this time I often find a song in my heart that I have never heard before and as I sing it I can often physically feel the subtle changes in energy. These 'spirit songs' are tunes that often I cannot remember after the ceremony. It is as if they are given to me to use in that moment and for that moment alone. I do not know whether they come from within me or from the spirit realm, but they have a unique energy about them and a power that is certainly outside of my normal experience. These songs seem to come only when the mind and body are on, with the ego well under control. If I say to myself, 'I want to sing a spirit song,' nothing comes into my mind; it is only when I allow myself to be carried by the energies of the circle and the guides and helpers I have called upon that these unique and powerful songs manifest.

At this time I also usually offer whatever prayers I feel are appropriate and these can be requests for help or guidance, healing prayers or more general prayers for peace in the world. Once again these prayers should come from the heart and not the ego. Prayers that begin with 'I want ...' or 'I desire ...' come from the ego and will not be answered in the way you want. The power of prayers and requests within the sacred circle is very strong so you must be careful what you wish for. Try to be specific in personal requests keeping in mind that what you ask for needs to fit harmoniously with your unfolding path of destiny. I often find that prayers come to mind at this time and so I never bother rehearsing what I am going to say beforehand, I just follow the guidance of the energies of the circle.

Once you feel you have done all you need to, spend some time in quiet meditation allowing your mind to be open to any guidance or messages from the spirit realm. This is often a time when I get new insights and understandings or am given a vision as a metaphorical answer to one or more of my prayers. If this occurs I make a mental note of them so that I can write them down after the ceremony. Finally, thank all the energies that have come to help you and break the circle either by walking around it anticlockwise or by stepping out in one of the cardinal directions. This forms the basis of many of my ceremonies, but you will find that the more you do, the more you are guided as to how to create your own, unique ceremonies. I have found that every ceremony is different and unique whether performed on my own or with other people. Once you make a true connection with the land, you will find that the energy of a ceremony is most often guided by what is happening in creation at that time, especially the phase of the moon and the season.

Solitary ceremonies are an excellent way to begin to reconnect with the land but, as you progress, you will naturally attract likeminded people into your life and may well feel led to join with them in ceremony. These can be very magical and potentially lifechanging experiences. Each person brings their own unique 'medicine' and power and, when these energies combine together, cemented by unconditional love and a desire to do only what is good and right, amazing things can happen. The power of combined voices in songs, prayers and chants creates a wonderful ball of positivity and beauty that can have a real and tangible effect, not only on those within the circle, but also on the community and land around. When several people combine their intents and focus upon healing, miracles can happen.

Working with others not only creates powerful, positive energies but it unites people together creating a foundation of mutual respect for one another and for each individual's uniqueness. Once you have shared ceremony with another person, a sacred bond is created that links you to that person for ever. I find that I can do ceremony with someone and not see him or her again for years, but when we do meet it is as if we've never been apart. Some of the most amazing ceremonies I have experienced have been when the participants have come from many different points in the spectrum of life. I have held ceremonies with participants ranging in age from seven to seventy and coming from many nationalities and traditions. The bond of love and mutual respect created in these ceremonies is humbling and brings a real sense of hope. If we can all learn to reconnect, then peace and harmony in the world becomes a possibility.

Here is the basic pattern for setting up a sacred circle.

~ CLEANSE AND PURIFY ~
sweep with birch broom, feather and/or incense
~ SET YOUR INTENT ~
with a prayer, asking for only positive energies to come into the circle
~ GROUND YOUR ENERGY ~
physically connect with the earth and visualise roots growing down from you into the earth
~ CAST THE CIRCLE ~
sunwise, using salt, grain or tobacco sprinkled from the right hand
~ ENTER AND COMPLETE THE CIRCLE ~
~ CALL IN POSITIVE ENERGIES ~
guides, animal energies, plant elementals, and so on
~ HONOUR THE ENERGIES ~
with singing, dancing, chanting, drumming
~ MAKE INTERCESSIONS ~
offer prayers and wishes for harmony and healing and meditate for answers and insights
~ THANK THE ENERGIES AND CLOSE THE CIRCLE ~

The use of colour in ceremony

The Celts understood that every colour in the universe has its own vibration and energy that can be harnessed to help us in our ceremonial work. Celtic mythology is full of colour symbolism and adding colour to a ceremony can dramatically change the tone of the energies in that ceremony. We often use different colours in the form of pieces of material or flowers to represent the seven directions and sometimes wear certain colours to set the mood of the ceremony. Below are some of the colours and the symbolism that the Celts associated with them.

Colour	Symbolism
Black	Earth, North, winter, death/rebirth, introspection, protection
Yellow	Air, East, spring, mental abilities, enlightenment, understanding, knowledge, healing
White	Fire, South, summer, divine semen, purity, truth, hope, harmony, clarity, protection
Red	Water, West, autumn, menstrual blood, love, passion, enthusiasm, courage
Green	Grandmother Earth, animal and plant energies, abundance, healing
Blue	Grandfather Sky, spirit guides, serenity, peace, intuition, the moon, meditation
Purple	the Great Spirit, creator, spirituality, higher consciousness
Brown	strength, stability, earthiness
Orange	energy, vitality, optimism, positivity, centredness
Pink	unconditional love, acceptance, friendship, caring, tenderness
Silver	the triple goddess, the moon, feminine power
Gold	spiritual authority, the sun, masculine power

Altered states of consciousness

There is often talk about altered states of consciousness in connection with shamanism and ceremony. What exactly does this
mean? An altered state of consciousness is exactly what it says, a
different perception of reality from that of normal, waking consciousness. Such states allow us to view the universe from a new
perspective, which can provide insights and solutions to problems
that are not available to the mind in its normal conscious state. It
allows us to communicate with animal, plant and stone energies
and to gain wisdom from them.

To understand this fully we need to once again look at the
human brain and the different vibrations of brainwaves that exist
in different states of consciousness. When we are in a normal,
waking state, our brain produces *beta* waves at a vibration of
about 21 Hz. A person in a high state of anxiety can show *beta*
brainwaves as high as 34 Hz and someone very relaxed can show
waves as low as 14 Hz. Once the brainwave vibration goes below
14 Hz we enter *alpha* state. *Alpha* waves range in vibration from
8 to 13 Hz and occur when we are meditating, daydreaming or in
a creative state of mind. This is also the normal brainwave pattern
of most animals. This is why, to communicate with animals, we
need to be in an *alpha* state of mind. If the vibration of brainwaves goes below 8 Hz we enter *theta* state. *Theta* waves range
from 4 to 7 Hz and occur in states of deep meditation, hypnosis,
trance and sleep. This is also the brainwave frequency for
shamanic activity such as shapeshifting and travelling to other
realms. It is the vibration of most trees and plants and is the
pattern one needs to achieve in order to fully communicate with
plant elemental energies. When the mind is producing *theta*
waves, solid objects start to look transparent and the mind can be
open to powerful levels of suggestibility. The trick is to reach this
state of consciousness whilst remaining aware of everything that
is happening. If this is mastered it can provide many powerful
insights and understandings.

There is a fourth brainwave pattern, *delta* waves, whose vibration goes from 0.5 to 4 Hz. They usually only occur in states of

deep sleep but can also occur during deep meditation or healing. In this state, the dimensions of space and time become interchangeable and it is no longer possible to distinguish between sight, feeling and sound. *Delta* waves also occur in advanced shamanic travel when shamans visit other dimensions and are also needed in communication with the energies of stones. It takes much training and self-control to achieve this last state of mind whilst remain consciously aware of all that is going on. It is not something that everyone can do and it can be potentially dangerous to those who are not grounded and connected to the energies of the land.

Working with ceremony

Making ceremony a part of your life changes your perspective on things. Whenever you feel 'stuck' or cannot find a way to proceed, performing ceremony is an excellent way to move the energies on. When I first started doing ceremony, I worked alone following my intuition and the more ceremony I performed, the more I learnt. From simple solitary ceremonies I have progressed to larger gatherings always working through my intuition and with unconditional love. As I have learnt to respect the land and my brothers and sisters on the path of life, so my own self-respect has risen and encouraged me to search for a still deeper understanding of this magical world we live in. I now recognise that there is no good or bad in the world until we interact with things and that everything has a positive and negative side. Performing ceremony sets you on a path to finding the positive and, consequently, health, happiness and fulfilment.

Before I started on this path I was addicted to cigarettes, smoking up to forty cigarettes per day. I had tried to give up on numerous occasions and failed every time. I even used to set myself up for a fall by announcing to all my friends that I was giving up only to publicly humiliate myself in front of them by failing a few days or even hours later. What I did not understand then was that I was using tobacco as a crutch because I was not happy in my life. Then one day I met a Native American who told me that to his people the tobacco was sacred and known as a 'teacher-plant'. He said it had great teachings to offer those who could learn to listen to them and could provide great healing. This confused me because everything I had read or heard about tobacco was saying how bad it was for your health and well-being. I resolved to try to understand this man's perspective.

At that time I was just beginning to work with ceremony and had witnessed some people using tobacco as an offering. I decided to perform my own ceremony to honour the spirit of the tobacco and ask it to teach me its wisdom. The ceremony was very simple and involved me breaking open my cigarettes and offering the tobacco to the seven directions followed by a simple prayer. Although the ceremony was very simple, my intent was pure and that made it very powerful. Almost immediately the spirit of tobacco began to teach me. The first thing I learnt was to stop trying to give it up. I came to the realisation that all the time I was unhappy with my life, I would not be able to give up tobacco. Instead of trying and repeatedly failing to give it up, I stopped fighting my addiction, accepted it and started actively seeking my own happiness. Shortly afterwards I became friends with a young man who taught me that cigarettes were full of additives, but that there were some hand-rolling tobaccos that were virtually additive-free and he said that having smoked both he found that the hand-rolling tobacco caused him less health problems. It seemed to make sense to me so I went to the shop where he bought it and purchased some myself.

It took me some time to learn to roll cigarettes for myself and I frequently became frustrated and reverted back to ready-made ones but, every time I did ceremony, I only ever used the natural tobacco. Eventually I converted totally to rolling my own cigarettes and then one day I had an amazing insight. I was in the middle of a ceremony and decided to roll myself a cigarette to honour and ask for teaching from the spirit of the tobacco as I had done many times before. This time, however, the spirit of the tobacco spoke clearly to me as if I was being spoken to by someone standing next to me. I must have inadvertently shifted my brainwave pattern into *theta* waves enabling me to have direct communication with the energy of the plant. The message was a mixture of images and words, emotions and sensations.

This was the message the spirit of the tobacco gave me:

> I come to teach humankind the meaning of respect. You humans have forgotten how to respect yourselves and creation. This is why you become addicted to cigarettes and why they cause you such ill health. The only way you can be free from this addiction is by taking your power back and the only way you can do this is by learning the ways of honour and respect. The illness comes from within your own minds, not from me; I only act as a catalyst to make you see the error of your ways. But so many of you even when faced with death, arrogantly refuse to see this truth.

Then I was shown a vision of how tobacco works with humans. First I was shown a vision of myself rolling a cigarette and whilst I was rolling I was saying prayers into the cigarette. With each prayer the tobacco took on a new colour until it was a rainbow of beautiful energy. I then lit the cigarette and saw all the energy centres in my body were glowing with colour. At the same time the rainbow of colours that were my prayers travelled out to the universe with each exhalation. Next I saw the smoke from the tobacco change into a pure white mist and as it entered my lungs it formed tiny crystals on the wall of my lungs that melted like ice and were absorbed in a few seconds. Next I was shown the smoke from a ready-made cigarette that was being smoked by a friend of mine who was also taking part in the ceremony. The smoke from his cigarette was not so white and as it entered his lungs it formed tiny pieces of silver that took days to be absorbed.

This vision changed my whole attitude to tobacco. I began rolling every cigarette with ceremony quietly filling it with positive thoughts and prayers even when I was smoking socially with friends. They were not aware that I was rolling with ceremony, to them I was just concentrating on the job in hand, but in my mind I was for the first time honouring my every interaction with this sacred plant. Shortly after this I was in a restaurant with friends having a meal. At the end of the meal I felt like having a cigarette and so decided that I would ask the waiter for an ashtray and roll myself one in the manner I had been shown in my vision. I called the waiter over and gave him my request to which he informed me that I was sitting in a non-smoking area and would have to move away from my friends to a table by the bar if I wanted to smoke. I decided that I would prefer to continue to share in the good time I was having with my friends rather than smoke on my own. This was the first time I had been able to make such a decision. Before I would have always chosen to leave my friends for a smoke and I suddenly realised — I was no longer an addict.

Today I still smoke, but only when the spirit of the tobacco calls to me and, when it does, I only ever smoke cigarettes that I have made myself in a sacred manner. I fill each one with positive prayers and wishes and always ask the energy of this powerful plant to open my mind and teach me new insights. Some days I may smoke five cigarettes and then I may not smoke for another five days or even weeks. I now understand that to be able to learn from this powerful teacher plant you must treat it with the utmost respect and this can only be achieved if you have the utmost respect for yourself. I never use tobacco to make myself feel better if I am in a bad headspace. I change my thinking first to one of harmony and balance and only then might I roll a cigarette to cement that connection. In this way, I hold on to my power by relying only on the strength of my own mind and the guidance of my intuition to show me how to be happy, healthy and fulfilled. This is just one of the many teachings that living ceremonially has given me. Every ceremony gives insights and understandings and takes us ever closer to our true, spiritual identity.

Nine

THE CELTIC SWEATLODGE

The use of sweatlodges in Britain dates back at least as far as the Celts and possibly beyond. Their form and structure varies from area to area but they all share similar symbolism and purpose. They also share striking similarities to the Native American sweatlodge and both generally take the following form.

A fire pit is created to house a sacred fire and, next to it, facing one of the four cardinal directions, is erected a simple altar. On the other side of the altar a roundhouse of hazel or willow poles is built with four doorways, one in each of the cardinal directions. The doorway nearest the altar is the usual door of entry and its orientation depends upon the energies you wish to work with:

- A door that opens towards the East represents Air and makes the sweatlodge primarily a place of learning and communicating with creation.
- A door that opens towards the South represents Fire and makes the lodge primarily a place where people can freely express their emotions and receive guidance and empowerment in the pursuit of their destiny.
- A door that opens towards the West represents Water and makes the lodge primarily a place of healing where people can be spiritually nourished and uplifted.
- A door that opens towards the North represents Earth and makes the lodge primarily a place of death and rebirth allowing one to let go of the past and embrace the future.

The lodge was traditionally covered in animal hides, though today we use tarpaulin and canvas, and is made impervious to all outside light. A central stone pit is dug and the doorway nearest the fire remains open whilst the fire and stones are prepared. The fire is built in a sacred manner, with a wide base upon which is placed a number of stones. The number of stones varies from ten to over fifty depending upon the ceremony although the average is twenty-eight. A fire is then built around the stones and, once offerings of salt, tobacco and herbs are placed upon it and appropriate prayers said, it is lit with a single match. Someone is in charge of firekeeping and it is their job to make sure that the stones are always covered whilst they are heating and to pass the stones into the lodge when they are ready. Whilst the fire is heating the stones, there is singing, drumming and dancing to build up the energies and to honour the spirits that have been called upon to help with the ceremony. After about two hours the participants are cleansed with herbs and enter the lodge. Red-hot stones are then passed by the firekeeper into the lodge on a pitchfork, collected by the leader of the lodge in a pair of antlers and placed in the central pit. When the appropriate number of stones have been taken into the lodge, it is closed so that all outside light is gone and only the glow of the stones remains. Herbs are put on the stones and water poured on so that the lodge fills with hot, aromatic steam. This is accompanied by appropriate prayers, songs and chants. When the moment feels right, the leader calls for the door to be opened and the round ends.

There are usually four rounds. Each round entails bringing a number of hot stones into the lodge, closing up the lodge and offering herbs, water, prayers, and so on. Traditionally in the first round the leader calls upon the energies of the four directions to bring balance and harmony to the lodge and the other participants call upon whatever energies or spirits are special to them. These can be spirit guides, power animals, plant elementals or stone beings and each are welcomed by pouring water upon the stones. Songs and chants are then sung to honour the energies and the ceremony unfolds in its own unique way. The second round is usually a healing round where participants can let go of pain and negative emotions. In the sweats I run we usually have a primal scream in this round to cleanse ourselves and express our energy. The third round is a prayer round where prayers and dreams are sent out to the universe and the fourth round is a closing round where the energies are thanked and honoured for their teachings.

The actual lodge symbolises the womb of Mother Earth and the fire the divine spark of the Creator. The stones, usually volcanic in origin (basalt, for example, does not shatter when heated and then dowsed with water), are heated in the fire so as to release their stored wisdom. This wisdom has always been regarded by the Celts as the most ancient and deep of all wisdoms. The four elements are represented as follows:

- Earth — the stones
- Air — the smoke and steam
- Fire — the sacred fire
- Water — the blessed water poured upon the stones.

As the steam rises so too does the wisdom of the stones and, as it condenses and rains down from the roof of the lodge, so those within are bathed in that wisdom. The leader of the lodge is the one who holds and balances all the energies making sure that every participant is safe and supported. Each lodge is different and unique depending upon the time of year, the energies of the participants and the intent with which it is prepared. Some are very hot and strong, others are cool and gentle but every lodge is exactly what it needs to be. It is like a death and rebirth experience and every participant comes out of the lodge a different person with new understandings, even if they are not always consciously aware of them.

Debbie and I hold sweatlodges to mark all the Celtic festivals and other important times like New and Full Moons and eclipses. We also hold them if someone needs a healing ceremony or if we feel that we need to initiate powerful change in our lives. Our friend Eli usually keeps fire and we collect wood and stones by hand from local sources. The wood comes only from fallen trees and the stones from a disused quarry in the middle of ancient woodland. It takes a great deal of hard work to collect, saw and chop the wood and to carry heavy stones through the woodland but Eli and I now make it a regular part of our preparation for ceremony. A week before a major sweat we go out and, after making offerings to the spirits of the land, saw up and wheelbarrow the wood or stones to the road to be placed in a trailer and driven home. Come rain or shine, summer or winter, we go out and are always rewarded for our efforts with powerful sweatlodges and wonderful gifts from the creator. With ceremony as with life, the more effort and intent you put into them, the greater your rewards. Many people do not realise this simple truth and often when I am holding a large sweatlodge, several participants will turn up just minutes before we are due to enter the lodge. They have missed the preparation and do not understand that in doing so have robbed themselves of many opportunities for insights and blessings.

The sweatlodge is a place of powerful and profound healing, but should also be a place of fun. There are some people who make up all sorts of rules to govern their sweatlodges but rules only serve to restrict people and stop them from expressing themselves freely. I have heard of rules such as 'everyone must enter the lodge naked' which of course makes a certain amount of sense as entering a lodge is like entering the womb but many people still have issues around nudity and if you make this a hard and fast rule you exclude many people from the lodge. Other rules I have heard include no singing in the lodge (for fear of accidentally singing a death chant and killing everyone!) and never entering through the North door (again for fear of death). Rules like these only serve to show the imbalance of the leader and to instil fear and thus create control over the participants. To me sweatlodges are places of freedom, not restriction; they are places to lose one's fears rather than gain new ones. If you enter a lodge with honour and respect, follow your intuition and come from a place of love, you can do no harm and no harm will come to you.

Your intuition is the voice of your higher-self guiding you and is never wrong. Sometimes intuition can lead you on some interesting learning experiences and many people lose faith in their own intuition because they fail to see the importance of lessons in their lives. They are looking for a comfortable life instead of a happy one and, when their intuition leads them down a road where they have to face their inner selves, they shy away and stop listening to it. But your intuition is your most powerful tool on the path of life. Each and every day it will show you omens and signs to guide you through life if you can only learn to truly look and listen.

Some years ago I was invited to join with a Native American medicine man at a gathering in Dorset. I was very new to the medicine path at that time but had had a number of visions one of which I shared with the wise-woman Eliana. She in turn shared it with Dennis, the Native American medicine man who said that he felt I was the Celtic connection he had been looking for and asked if I would help lead a Celtic visualisation at the gathering. I consented, not really knowing what I was supposed to do, but I had already reached a point in my life where I followed my intuition and it felt right to say 'yes'. Eliana said to me that she would drum and guide the participants on a visualisation to a stone barrow where they would enter and meet Merlin. I was then supposed to speak as Merlin and say whatever I felt was appropriate.

In the weeks leading up to the gathering I read all I could about Merlin and tried to get an idea of what to say. When the gathering finally came I was nervous but felt as ready as I ever would. When I arrived, Eliana said that her intuition was telling her that I should sit in one of the cardinal directions and lay out my medicine tools in front of me. I had some crystals, herbs and stones with me and I laid them neatly on a cloth in front of me. About forty people turned up and then Dennis arrived. I felt a stranger in the midst of many friends. I could see people looking at me wondering who I was and why I was sitting in one of the directions and I too was wondering the same. Dennis said, 'There are many people with many gifts gathered this day, although some, including Andy over there, do not even realise their own gifts.' Everyone's eyes turned to look at me and at that moment I was beginning to wonder just what I had got myself into.

Dennis then led us all in a visualisation and after a short break then went around the whole group interpreting everyone's visions. I was amazed at how much this man knew. It seemed that, whatever the picture created by each person during the visualisation, Dennis knew its meaning and was able to show clearly the lesson it was trying to teach each individual. I suddenly realised how little I knew and felt at that moment that it would take me years of study to get to the same level of knowledge as this man. That evening was my first experience of a Native American sweatlodge and the whole experience was like walking through a doorway into a new world. I had never before felt the power of group ceremony and for the first time in my life I had a real sense of belonging and inner peace. I entered the lodge a stranger and came out surrounded by friends.

The next day we gathered again and before I had time to wonder what was going to happen Dennis announced that I was going to lead a Celtic visualisation. Fear and panic gripped me but Eliana, sensing my trepidation, gently signalled me to join her in the centre of the circle and whispered some words of encouragement into my ear. She began the visualisation whilst I desperately rehearsed in my mind the words I had decided to say when it was my time to speak. She gently beat a drum and led the group on a magical journey to an ancient stone barrow. She told them to enter the barrow and then said, 'And before you stands the Merlin who turns to you and says ...' She signalled to me that it was my time to speak and at that moment everything I had rehearsed went straight out of my mind. I had no choice but to seek my intuition and as I did so a new set of words came into my mind.

I said exactly what my intuition told me to say and afterwards several people came up to me and said how powerful they had found the visualisation. Dennis said that we would break for lunch and afterwards do the interpretations. I felt relieved that it had gone so well and relaxed safe in the knowledge that this medicine man would have all the answers and interpretations to everyone's visions. I felt as if my job was done and decided that I did not need to be present during the interpretations and so went to help with the fire that was being built for another sweat-lodge that evening. When Dennis sent someone to get me I was somewhat confused as to why he should want me present whilst he interpreted other people's visions, but I went along and joined the circle of people.

As I entered the circle everyone's eyes fell on me and I felt a little self-conscious but tried to put it out of my mind. Then my worst nightmare became reality as Dennis announced that I was now going to give the interpretations to everyone's visions. At that moment I wished the ground would open up and swallow me. Here was a man, who appeared to me to know everything, asking me, who knew nothing, to interpret forty visions. Dennis could sense my panic and said in a gentle, reassuring voice, 'Just see how you get on and if you have any problems I'll help you out.' I said a quick prayer for help and as the first person told me what she had seen, I cleared my mind and opened up my intuition. To my surprise I knew exactly what her vision meant. The meaning popped into my head and I just said it. The same thing happened with the next person and the next one until I had gone round and interpreted everyone's vision.

Afterwards many of the people came up to me saying how much the interpretations had helped them and asking me how I had managed to accumulate such a vast knowledge of the meanings of colours and symbols. I tried to tell them that I knew nothing and had only listened to my intuition and the voice of spirit, but they seemed not to understand. Since then I have learnt to always follow my intuition and to be open to the omens and messages it shows me. I was placed in a situation where I as a human being was totally ill-equipped, but spirit was with me, as it is with everyone who learns to trust his or her inner voice and heed its wisdom. I have since realised that the answers to all ques-tions lie within each of us and that if we learn to let go of our egos and follow the voice of our intuition, we can find answers to every question our minds can possibly create. This is the power of the intuition that enables you to connect to higher spiritual energies for wisdom and guidance.

Once you learn to follow your intuition, every day becomes an adventure with new discoveries and insights; whether the day is challenging or easy, each one has its own lessons to teach. One of the most important things I have learnt whilst following a Celtic path is to expect the unexpected. Sometimes you are led to change all the 'rules' and such was the case when the time came for Debbie and me to celebrate the autumn equinox of 1999. We had planned as usual to hold a sweatlodge on the eve of the equinox and several friends had indicated that they would like to join us. I sensed that the sweat was going to be a particularly powerful one, especially as it was after a very powerful solar eclipse on 11 August. It also coincided with me writing this chapter so I sensed that whatever happened I would be sharing it with you as I am now.

About two days before we were due to sweat I had a vision. It showed me many things including a picture of how the energies of the land had been affected by the eclipse. The eclipse was thought by many to be primarily about the power of the sun but I sensed it was more about the power of the moon. When a solar eclipse occurs it is the moon that blocks out the light of the sun and thus has power over the sun. I was shown in my vision how this rise in the power of the moon initiated a rise in the power of the dark energies of the universe. Not only had the moon blotted out the light of the sun but, when it did, it was in its dark phase. This had caused many people to have a time of great difficulty both emotionally and physically immediately after the eclipse.

Debbie and I had felt this energy shift too and had experienced a very challenging month on many different levels. But it had not upset us or caused us great disharmony, as we have learnt to embrace such times with pleasure, recognising that hard times bring their own teachings. Besides, we know that everything comes to an end some time and we knew that this difficult phase would too; but we were both feeling rather drained by all the putting into perspective we'd had to do. My vision showed me that this dark time was important as it had initiated a process of letting go and dying to the past on a very deep level. It then showed me how to shift the energies so that we could walk back into the light and bring this process to completion. The autumn equinox is usually a time to honour the dark energies as the power of darkness takes ascendance over the light until the winter solstice arrives. Holding a sweat on the eve of the equinox welcomes those dark energies and usually marks the beginning of a time of great introspection for Debbie and me as we prepare for the Samhain ceremonies. But my vision told me to hold the sweat after the equinox. Two days after the equinox there was to be a Full Moon and my vision said that if we held the sweat the evening after the equinox and prior to the Full Moon we would attract the light energies of the moon into our lives. This in turn would make the next month brighter and easier for all who took part in the ceremony.

I was also shown that to make this shift from dark to light we had to first embrace the darkness without fear. I saw myself entering the sweat through the North door, something I had not done before, and that the first round of the ceremony should be held in complete darkness. After this we would open up the South door and this would bring in the power of the light from the fire. We would walk into darkness and emerge into light. Whenever I receive a vision I always question it to verify its truth. One must have faith in order to receive visions but one must also have doubt in order to discern the truth in them. I shared my vision with Debbie; she said that it felt right to her and, because it seemed also to make sense to me, we decided to follow its guidance.

We phoned our friends and told them that the date for the Herfest sweat had been moved to the Thursday night (the equinox being on the Thursday morning) and that they were still welcome to come if they were able. Several people could not make that evening but they were not upset because they understood that we would only change the night of the sweat at such short notice if we had a good reason. All our friends accept that if they are meant to do ceremony with us they will be there, and if they are not, they won't. They understand that the universe governs this and opens and closes doorways to guide us to where we should be at any time in our lives.

Over the next two days the manner in which the ceremony should be performed came more clearly into my mind. Whenever I receive a vision, there is always too much information for my conscious mind to take in and so it takes a few days for all the messages and images to filter down from my higher consciousness into my conscious mind. My vision told me to use some oats to make the shape of a pregnant goddess around the sweatlodge and fire. This would honour the land at this time of Herfest and also allow us to draw upon the energies of the goddess during our ceremony. The picture I saw was of her head encircling the fire and her body encircling the sweatlodge. This placed the North door at her genital area and the South door at her throat, meaning that we would enter the lodge through her vagina, into the womb, and would emerge through her mouth. This reminded me of the story of Cerridwen and Taliesin except that, instead of the goddess eating us and then giving birth to us, it would be in reverse. This again made sense because we were doing everything in reverse so that we could reverse and balance the influence of the dark energies and step out into the light.

On the morning of the sweat Eli telephoned. We had not spoken to him for several weeks, although this is not unusual because he does not have a phone. Eli lives in the middle of woodland in a giant hazel dome and this makes him hard to contact at times. He had phoned us several times from a call box and we had been up to his home but we kept missing each other. This morning, however, Eli had awoken with a very strong urge to phone us. I told him that we were doing ceremony that night and asked if he would like to keep fire. He said he'd love to and so I went and picked him up. Whenever Eli keeps fire for a ceremony I am running, we like to spend the day together. It helps us to make a stronger connection and this enables us to understand each other during the ceremony without having to speak to each other. We just read each other's energy and communicate mentally. This does not mean that we don't speak to each other during ceremony, but if I need his help to hold the energies of the sweat in the middle of a round, I know that he will be there for me. He'll sing, drum or give his energies to me in whatever way his intuition tells him without me needing to call for his help verbally.

Eli and I drove into town sharing tales of our recent adventures. He needed to buy rice for a fast he was planning the following week and I needed to buy a salmon. Another part of my vision had told me that it would be good for us to feast upon salmon after the sweat and that it should be cooked with nine hazel nuts (as in the Celtic legend of Fintan, the Salmon of Knowledge). After shopping we returned home and then took a trailer into the woods to collect firewood for the sweat that night. Normally we would not have needed to do this on the day but I had been busy writing so we had not had a chance to go out and collect wood earlier. I had sawn up some old fence-posts up that were given to me by the farmer next door but this was not enough for a full fire.

After that we had lunch with Debbie, then went our separate ways to prepare for the ceremony in our own manner. Eli always goes through a long cleansing ceremony before firekeeping, bathing himself in herbs and oils and meditating to clear his mind. Keeping fire is not a simple job and Eli has learnt that the cleaner you are in mind and body, the easier it is to hear the spirit of the fire. Fire demands respect and those who approach firekeeping with arrogance always get burnt. Eli is wiser than that and always goes through his own ceremony before keeping fire. Debbie's preparation and cleansing is much subtler and to many people goes unnoticed. To the untrained eye she goes around the house tidying here and there and generally cleaning. However, what she is actually doing is going around the whole house in a cleansing ceremony turning every piece of negative energy into beauty. This means that by the time our friends arrive, they come to a house that exudes peace and beauty. This is Debbie's gift that is both subtle and exceedingly powerful. I prepare in a different way by walking in my woods and communing with Nature.

It was a dull, showery day but this always makes the woods even more magical than usual because the rain highlights stones and wood, making them shine with colour. I love walking in the woods whatever the weather and, whenever I go for a walk, I always take with me my trusty blackthorn walking stick. It is now an old ally having been with me to many magical places and ancient sites; I always find it helps me to connect with the energy of the trees. As I walked that afternoon I tried to clear my mind of all thoughts and take my brainwave pattern down to a more meditative state. First I went to the only rowan tree in that particular wood and asked if it would give some of its berries to decorate our altar that night. At first I thought it would not yield any berries as the only ones I could see were far out of reach, but then it showed me a small bunch hidden under its leaves and it said I could take these. I thanked the tree and left it an offering of salt before pressing on.

Next I headed towards a sacred spring that I knew was close by and on the way came across the broken shell of an owl's egg. The owl is one of my guardian animals and I took this as an omen that the owl would visit our ceremony that night. When I arrived at the spring I asked its spirit if it would allow me to cleanse myself in its beautiful waters. The spring spirit, with whom I have had many encounters, consented and I offered some salt to it and then bathed my head in the fresh water that bubbled up from deep within the earth. Walking further into the woods I disturbed a squirrel gathering nuts, which I thought was poignant at Herfest time, and then I came across a clump of wild marjoram. I am familiar with the elemental energy of this plant and asked it if I could take a leaf to use for an additional cleansing. The spirit of the marjoram had told me some years ago that if you wipe your third eye, the psychic centre of the body on the forehead between the eyebrows, and your nose with a single fresh leaf, it opens up the senses and helps one to make a stronger connection with the woodland energies. The spirit told me I could take a single leaf and, after leaving an offering, I plucked the leaf that called out to me and wiped my third eye and nose with it. Almost immediately I caught sight of a piece of white stone and as I went over to pick it up I found that it was actually a piece of white crystal. My intuition told me that it would give me of its energy but that I should not take it out of the woodland so I placed it in my left hand and walked on.

As I walked the crystal felt very hot in my hand. It certainly seemed to be giving me some of its energy and I got the sensation that it, being made of stone, was helping to strengthen my connection to the stone people in preparation for the sweat. Then, as I continued walking, a hazel tree caught my eye. I first saw it out of my peripheral vision and had walked some distance past it before my conscious mind became aware of it. I turned to greet it and it seemed to be calling me over to it. I walked to it and around it and found another broken eggshell. This one was much smaller than the owl's shell I had found earlier and I did not recognise what bird it had come from. It reminded me though of the perpetual cycle of birth, life and death. It had not so long ago surrounded and protected a tiny, fragile chick and here it was now, discarded and forgotten returning back to Mother Earth. The chick would become an adult and produce its own eggs, and so the cycle goes on. My thoughts turned back to the sweat and an image of the ceremony became clearer in my mind. I saw the first round as a round without stones and in total darkness. This would be our own symbolic death where we would embrace everything without judgement. Then I saw myself lighting a blue candle to welcome in the power of the light and to honour the light of the moon. I walked on and came to an old chestnut tree that was already shedding its nuts. I greeted it and asked to take one of its prickly nut cases with me to decorate our altar that night. The tree said that it would make a change from squirrels taking them and that it would be honoured to give a little of itself to our ceremony.

A little later I arrived at the yew tree where I have an altar and stone circle. I greeted it as one does an old friend and talked to it of the ceremony I was leading that night. I placed the crystal on the altar thanking it for its energies and then went to the stone circle to make my offerings. I held salt up to each of the seven directions asking for the energies of land and sky to help and guide me in the ceremony. I then placed some salt on the altar to honour the spirit of the yew and walked round to the other side of the majestic old tree. On the other side, just above my head was a small hole in the side of it filled with moss. I put my hand in the hole and pulled out a plastic bag that I had put there some months ago. In it was a small sage stick given to me by Eli and I took it out and lit it. As I did so I called upon the spirit of the sage to cleanse and purify my body, mind and spirit. I wafted the smoking herbs around my head, down my back, under each foot and up my front. The scent of burning sage cut through the clean forest air like a knife bringing me clarity and focus. Then I heard the grandfather hazel tree calling me from across the forest and, after extinguishing the sage and placing it back in the bag and into the hole, I headed on.

When I arrived at the hazel, one of the oldest I had found in the forest, I went up to it as usual and greeted it. I told it about the ceremony that night and about my vision of the salmon. I asked if I could take nine of its nuts to which it replied that it was too old to bear fruit but that it would show me a younger tree on the path ahead that would give of its nuts. It was then that I spotted some wild woodruff and my intuition told me that I had seen it to remind me to bring its energy into the sweat. I thanked it for the reminder and continued on the path looking for the young hazel the grandfather tree had spoken of. I had not gone far when I came across a hazel laden with nuts. Two clusters of nuts called out to me and after asking permission I picked them. As I examined them I found that one cluster contained four nuts and the other five. I had my nine hazels and so headed home.

On the way out of the forest a single acorn called to be picked up as did an empty chestnut case that reminded me that the case in my pocket would soon yield its nuts and so continue its turning on the Wheel of Life. As I exited the forest I was greeted by the call of the crow, reminding me once more of the death and rebirth process that I and those doing ceremony with me would experience that night and, with that positive omen in my mind, I drove home. When I arrived home I chopped some wood for the fire and then Eli and I covered the sweat. Two friends of ours, Laura and Sue, arrived and we all began preparing the fire. Earlier that day Debbie, Eli and I had decided that thirty stones would be a good number to use and after asking Sue to lay the first stone I laid out seven stones, one in each of the directions. We each laid stones by picking them up, saying a simple prayer and then laying them upon a wooden base wherever our intuition told us to. Once all thirty stones were laid, Eli and I began covering them in paper and kindling. I then offered salt to the seven directions to bless the fire while Eli did the same with tobacco. The rain had stopped and there was a strong, gusting wind which we knew would help us once we got the fire lit, but that very wind made it hard to light the fire in the first place. It took three attempts and about seven matches to get the fire going. The kindling was rather damp and we were short of paper but, with perseverance and some drumming from Sue and me, we finally got it going. The wind fanned the flames and before long the fire was roaring. Sue and I continued to drum, Laura danced whilst Eli built the fire up until it was burning all the way round. Meanwhile Debbie was preparing the feast, filling it with her love and beauty whilst at the same time sending her energy to the fire.

Every sacred fire is unique, having its own character and nature. Some are hot and roaring whilst others are gentler in their heat and behaviour. This fire was wild and untamed. The swirling wind threw flames out in every direction making it difficult to put more wood onto it without getting a face full of flames. This did not concern Eli as he is well used to talking to and working with the fire spirits. When he keeps fire the flames and the stones within them both speak to him and show him where and when to lay wood and later instruct him which stones to take into the lodge. Keeping fire is as powerful and mystical an experience as going into a sweatlodge and it teaches one a new understanding and respect for fire. Those who approach the fire with force or arrogance get burnt whilst those who quickly learn that fire needs gentleness and respect emerge unscathed. Two hours later the stones were ready and so we got changed into sarongs and prepared to enter the lodge. Whilst we were standing by the fire the hoot of a nearby owl sounded and I knew it was time to enter.

I was told by my intuition that instead of cleansing ourselves with herbs before entering the lodge as we normally did, we should go in as we were. Debbie, Sue, Laura, Eli and I entered within the circle of oats by the fire and we each took a handful of oats to close the circle and offer to the fire. The three women and I entered through the North door and after we had got ourselves comfortable Eli closed it up so that we sat in pitch darkness. It was then that I realised I was sitting with the embodiment of the triple goddess. Laura, being young and unmarried represented the maiden, Sue being a mother represented the mother and Debbie, who had started her moon-time that morning, represented the Crone. Here I was once again doing ceremony with women only inside the sweat with me. This often happens and is how it should be: this is a time for women to connect with their power so that they can show men how to be truly empowered.

What actually happened within the sweat will remain only in the minds of those who were there but it was a truly magical experience. I can tell you that the darkness was warm and not the least bit frightening. After the first round we opened up the South door and I lit the candle. We then had nine stones for the second round because the number nine is the number of wisdom and is sacred to the dark goddess. Every stone was welcomed by us each rubbing them with herbs that filled the sweat with a beautiful smell. I used woodruff, Debbie sweetgrass, Laura *osha* root (a Native American herb) and Sue sage. The *osha* and sage were gifts to me from an Apache medicine man called Ernesto who had shared ceremony with us on the eclipse. In the third round we had ten stones to represent the transition from wisdom to the rebirth of enlightenment — '10' is made up of '1' and '0' which when added together make 1, the number of the sun and rebirth — and in the fourth round we had the other eleven stones, which is the number of revelation and insight. It was hot within the sweat but not unbearable. We sang songs, beat drums, chanted, prayed, meditated and at times just sat in the silence and the darkness being at one with both. We all came out shining and renewed and afterwards feasted upon the salmon poached with seasonal vegetables and nine hazelnuts, three-seed bread and organic brown rice cooked with a little wild red and long grain rice.

So came the end of another sacred ceremony and the next day each of us felt the shift in energy. Life turned another corner, the wheel moved on and we ran with its motion, in harmony with the universe around us. This sweat, however, made me feel as if I was surfing on top of the dark energies rather than being immersed in them. Everything felt good and right and I saw that the ceremony changed the way we interacted with the energies of the land just as I had seen in my vision. The vision had been fulfilled and could now become part of our accumulated wisdom; thus, we all walk onwards and upwards on the spiral of life.

This is the reality in which I live as I follow a Celtic path. It allows me to walk freely in two worlds and to interact with the energies of both. I work as any other person does. I have bills to pay, a family to grow and learn with, difficulties and challenges to overcome and everything else that goes with living in the western world. However, I also live a magical life where I have conversations with the energies of plants, trees, animals, stones and spirits. When the modern world gets tough, I do not retreat into the other world to escape reality; I enter it in order to draw inspiration and to increase my understanding, always doing so whilst understanding my need to return to the modern world. Both worlds are part of the same universe and both are subject to the same fundamental laws. What I learn in one serves me in the other, and vice versa. I now understand the Wheel of Life and how to flow with it and turn it into a spiral of learning.

Some people say to me, 'I like what you teach and how you view the world Andy, but it isn't real.' To them I always reply that it is real to me. Debbie and I have fashioned a life that is as real as any other. To many people we are a bit strange, perhaps even weird, especially when we say we cannot go to some social function because we have to do ceremony. But we have an exciting and wonderfully fulfilling life together. We embrace everything with pleasure because we understand that it is we who dictate what is good and what is bad by how we interact with life. The Celts believed that you reap what you sow and I know this to be true. If you have a life full of anger and resentment, if your thoughts are not pure and beautiful, then you will attract the same chaotic energy into your life. But, if you always think beautiful thoughts and do everything 100 per cent, seeking nothing in return except the pleasure of doing it, you will have a life full of beauty and pleasure. This is the way to honour both yourself and creation and is the key to walking the Wheel of Life. Do not judge what comes into your life; seek only to learn from it without prejudice. In this way, your life will be an adventure full of un-expected delights and insights. Your life will not be easy, but it will be fun. An easy life is a dull life and does little for the growth of the soul. A hard life that is embraced with pleasure builds the soul and the spirit so that there is nothing that you fear and no adversity over which you cannot rise. The past is gone and the future unwritten, here and now, moment by moment you create your own reality. Understand the Wheel of Life and you will under-stand the meaning of life and how to get the very best from it.

May the light of the sun ever inspire you,
The wind blow strong on your back to urge you ever onwards,
The power of the goddess and the moon uplift you and
May you walk forever onwards and upwards with beauty and respect for all.

Blessed be.

BIBLIOGRAPHY AND FURTHER READING

Aburrow, Yvonne, *The Enchanted Forest*, Berkshire: Capall Bann 1993

Aburrow, Yvonne, *Auguries and Omens*, Berkshire: Capall Bann 1994

Baggott, Andy, *Celtic Wisdom*, London: Piatkus Books 1999

Baggott, Andy, *Runes*, Anness Publishing 1999

Baggott, Andy, *Dream Power*, Hants: Godsfield Press 2000

Bord, Janet and Colin, *The Enchanted Land*, London: Thorsons 1995

Carr-Gomm, Philip and Stephanie, *The Druid Animal Oracle*, London: Eddison Sadd 1994

Davies, Marion, *Sacred Celtic Animals*, Berkshire: Capall Bann 1998

Devereux, Paul, *Places of Power*, London: Blandford 1990

Dixon-Kennedy, Mike, *Celtic Myth and Legend*, London: Blandford 1996

Ferguson, Diana, *The Magickal Year*, London: Batsford 1996

Green, Marion, *A Calendar of Festivals*, Dorset: Element Books 1991

Green, Miranda, *Animals in Celtic Life and Myth*, London: Routledge 1992

Hawkins, Gerald S., *Stonehenge Decoded*, London: Fontana 1970

Heaney, Marie, *Over Nine Waves — A Book of Irish Legends*, London: Faber and Faber 1994

Hole, Christina, *British Folk Customs*, London: Hutchinson 1976

Mann, Nicholas R., *The Keltic Power Symbols*, Sussex: Triskele 1987

McDonald, Lorraine, *Celtic Totem Animals*, Isle of Arran: Clan Dalraida 1992

Newman, Paul, *Lost Gods of Albion*, Stroud: Sutton Publishing 1997

Pennick, Nigel, *Celtic Sacred Landscapes*, London: Thames and Hudson 1996

Rolleston, T. W., *Celtic Myths and Legends*, London: Senate 1994

Squire, Charles, *Mythology of the Celtic People*, London: Bracken Books 1996

Walker, Barbara G., *The Women's Encyclopædia of Myths and Secrets*, London: Harper Collins 1983